MW00653738

TO MAKE A KILLING

TO MAKE A KILLING

Arthur Cutten, the Man Who Ruled the Markets

ROBERT STEPHENS

McGill-Queen's University Press

Montreal & Kingston | London | Chicago

© McGill-Queen's University Press 2024

ISBN 978-0-2280-2030-1 (cloth)
ISBN 978-0-2280-2031-8 (ePDF)

Legal deposit first quarter 2024
Bibliothèque nationale du Québec

Printed in Canada on acid-free paper that is 100% ancient forest free
(100% post-consumer recycled), processed chlorine free

We acknowledge the support of the Canada Council for the Arts.

Nous remercions le Conseil des arts du Canada de son soutien.

McGill-Queen's University Press in Montreal is on land which
long served as a site of meeting and exchange amongst Indigenous
Peoples, including the Haudenosaunee and Anishinabeg nations. In
Kingston it is situated on the territory of the Haudenosaunee and
Anishinaabek. We acknowledge and thank the diverse Indigenous
Peoples whose footsteps have marked these territories on which
peoples of the world now gather.

Library and Archives Canada Cataloguing in Publication

Title: To make a killing : Arthur Cutten, the man who ruled the
    markets / Robert Stephens.
Names: Stephens, Robert (President of PR Post), author.
Description: Includes bibliographical references and index.
Identifiers: Canadiana (print) 20230524737 | Canadiana (ebook)
    20230524826 | ISBN 9780228020301 (cloth) | ISBN 9780228020318
    (ePDF)
Subjects: LCSH: Cutten, Arthur, 1870-1936. | LCSH: Capitalists and
    financiers—United States—Biography. | LCSH: Grain trade—
    United States—History—20th century. | LCGFT: Biographies.
Classification: LCC HG172.C88 S74 2024 | DDC 332.6092—dc23

Set in 10/14 Radiata with Goldenbook
Book design & typesetting by Garet Markvoort, zijn digital

To Sally

For Everything You Are

CONTENTS

FIGURES

ACKNOWLEDGMENTS

Many people and organizations helped me with the research into Arthur Cutten's life. It was not an easy task as Cutten, ever secretive, covered his tracks well. Special thanks therefore to: Jim Nelson Jr for his memories of Cutten's country estate; Ted Shirley, grandson of Joseph Shirley (Arthur Cutten's nephew); Nigel McMurray for information about Frank O. Salisbury's painting of Cutten; Carol Wandschneider of the Downers Grove Historical Society; the Forest Preserve District of DuPage County; Guelph Museums; Guelph Public Library; Cutten Fields; Carole Stuart with the Collingwood Public Library; Archives of Ontario; Chicago History Museum; General Motors Heritage Center; Library of Congress, Prints and Photographs Division; and Hagley Museum and Library.

I'd also like to thank the team at McGill-Queen's University Press for believing in this project and for their help in bringing it to life, especially Richard Baggaley, Kathleen Fraser, Joanne Richardson, and Jacqui Davis.

Every effort was made to contact copyright owners to obtain the appropriate permissions for publication. If anyone has been inadvertently omitted, please contact the author at robert@outlawvoice.com.

TO MAKE A KILLING

PROLOGUE

What they said about Arthur Cutten ...

"Not only the most daring, but the most unerring speculator the world has ever known." James A. Patten, friend, mentor, and fellow trader.

"One of the most glamourous figures in speculative history." Edward Jerome Dies, author of *Street of Adventure*.

"As famous on Wall Street as Babe Ruth and Ty Cobb were in baseball." Robert Sobel, author of *Inside Wall Street*.

"The greatest speculator this country has ever had." Leo Tierney, counsel for the US Grain Futures Administration.

"There was magic – in those days – in the name of Cutten." Ferdinand Pecora, chief counsel to the US Senate Committee on Banking and Currency.

One hundred years ago, America was entering one of the wildest, most spectacular decades in its history, the Roaring Twenties. It was a period of unprecedented growth and mass consumerism. Old conventions of thrift, prudence, and moderation were cast aside. In the New Era, people bought on the instalment plan – radios, appliances, automobiles – drank in speakeasies, danced to jazz, idolized gangsters and movie stars, and bet their future on the stock market. They were in a hurry to have it all.

Arthur Cutten was their hero. He amassed a fortune in the grain pits and on the stock exchange, and his every move was followed closely by those wanting to ride on his coattails. His fabulous market winnings, estimated at $100 million (equivalent to $1.5 billion today), put him in a league of his own.

Born and raised in a small town in Canada, Cutten went to Chicago in 1890 with ninety dollars in his pocket. He was there to seek his fortune. But there was also another, darker motivation: he was determined to win back what his disgraced father had lost.

With utter ruthlessness, he conducted corners and bear raids, buying and selling more wheat and corn than anyone before, millions of bushels at a time. On Wall Street, he manipulated prices through syndicates and pools, engaged in wash trading (simultaneously buying and selling a security to attract investor interest), traded on insider information, and promoted shares to a gullible public. Anyone could get rich quick. All you had to do was follow this new Midas.

When the Crash came in 1929, when the good times turned bad, the heroes of prosperity became the culprits of the Great Depression. Aiming to whip up public support for new securities legislation, the Roosevelt administration launched an all-out attack on the "banksters." At the top of the list was Arthur Cutten. A US Senate committee probed his stock market practices, the Grain Futures Commission moved to bar him from the pits, and the Bureau of Internal Revenue indicted him for income tax evasion.

Cutten spent the remainder of his life fighting government. The wily operator won on every count, scoring a landmark victory in the Supreme Court, and even cheating the feds in death. When his estate was probated, the tax collectors were stunned to find that his vast wealth had disappeared. Certain that he had secreted his money out of the country, the authorities spent years searching for his treasure. It was never found.

This is the true story of a man who played by his own rules, beat the odds, and became one of the richest market operators in America. It is an account of the legendary figure who was credited with leading the Great Bull Market and then reviled for plunging the nation into misery and ruin with the collapse of stock prices.

This first in-depth biography of Arthur Cutten tells the tale of his grand adventures, examines the forces that propelled him, and introduces the cast of characters who inhabited his world. Today, there are many unnerving parallels with his times: volatile stock market prices, rising trade tariffs, ballooning household debt, the emergence of disruptive new technologies, the cult of celebrity, and an impatient lust for fortune.

He pulled the levers, and the markets, spellbound, moved to his commands. *To Make a Killing* unravels his secrets and exposes the man behind the curtain.

CHAPTER ONE

A Strange Dream

Chicago, May 1936.

Propped up in bed in his suite at the Drake Hotel, the old man lived in a world of luxury. His minions looked after him. His every need was attended to. He was rich, he was successful. And he was dying.

No amount of wealth could delay the inevitable. His doctors had declared that his chronic heart condition was incurable. He had known this for many years, but it had always seemed distant, with time enough before the clock ran out. Then a heart attack the previous December had brought death to his door. It could not be bought off or traded away for all his millions.

Through the window, he could see the summer clouds scuttling above the blue expanse of Lake Michigan. He was tired, and his pallid face and grey hair seemed to dissolve into the white pillows that supported him. His thin body lay beneath sheets and blankets. An oxygen bottle stood by the bed.

His nurse, Ethel Dickinson, brought his lunch into the room. He had no appetite. His wife Maud came by. He had no wish to talk.

His failing health was a subject of constant news coverage. A death watch was on: "Mr. Cutten will never be strong enough again to take up trading. He is just going to rest from now on," his wife announced in a press statement.[1] "Arthur W. Cutten, who rose from bookkeeper to become one of the world's greatest grain speculators, is through with the market," the Associated Press reported.[2]

A few weeks shy of his sixty-sixth birthday, he could rightly claim that he had achieved almost everything he had put his mind and soul to – he had beaten his opponents, made a financial killing, survived the Great Depression, and escaped the inquisitions of government.

But what he loved most – playing and winning in the great game of the markets – was now beyond his waning powers. He had often thought of himself as a prize fighter,[3] taking terrific blows in a ring where only the strongest and most iron-willed survived. And he had triumphed as the undisputed champion in the grain pits of Chicago and the stock exchange of New York. But he was done now. The glory days were gone.

At the usual hour Dr Arthur Byfield appeared, sitting at the bedside, checking blood pressure and other vitals. Later, he could hear them talking in hushed tones in the hallway.

How had he arrived at this moment and place? It seemed a strange dream, like it was only yesterday that he had come to this city, lacking money and influence.[4]

He shut his eyes and drifted off. A strange dream indeed.

Guelph, Ontario, Canada. Half a century earlier.

He woke with a start, bounced out of bed, and threw on his clothes. Late for school. Running downstairs, he was confronted by his father who waited impatiently at the kitchen table. Reaching into his vest, the elder Cutten withdrew a pocket watch and tapped the timepiece. Arthur knew to get moving. A few gulps of oatmeal, and he was out the door. His books were tied together by a leather strap, slung over his back, and his snap-brimmed hat was pushed back on his head.

Outside, he almost collided with the washerwoman who was just now arriving for work at the Cutten household. "Beg your pardon, Queen Esther. Good morning, ma'am," he called as he rushed past. She watched him until he disappeared, shaking her head and chuckling at the busy affairs of this boy.

He ran along Paisley to Yorkshire Street, where the Guelph Collegiate Institute was located. It was only a block away, but he was already late. The building was L-shaped with a tower at the outer corner. Principal William Tytler's office was located in the tower, and above it was a room used as a library. The main wing housed four classrooms on the first floor and a large assembly hall above. There was no plumbing, and the building was heated by fireplaces. A pump provided drinking water. A double row of privies stood outside.

Arthur snuck into his class and took a seat at the back. The teacher, James Davidson, noted the late arrival but decided to let it go. Arthur, after all, was one of his best pupils. "Bulls and bears, futures and crop futures didn't mean a thing to young Art Cutten in the days when he rolled a hoop along Paisley Street and rubbed its muddy rim all over his clean, white shirt," observed *Maclean's* magazine. "But he was good at arithmetic, Mr. Davidson said, and one may believe it."[5]

On another occasion, he ran afoul of the principal himself. Rather than attending to his studies, Arthur was playing with a mirror, catching the sunlight and reflecting it about the classroom. The other students were snickering at this distraction. Suddenly, he felt a strong grip at the back of his neck. Dr Tytler had come up from behind. He seized the boy and shook him.[6] Chastened and red-faced, Arthur bowed his head and buried his nose in his books. Discipline was restored.

Arthur William Cutten, born 6 July 1870, was always a bit of a loner, even as kid. He was shy and socially awkward, although intensely loyal to his pals. Serious, smart, a whiz with numbers. He was also known to play hooky from time to time, going with his friends to the swimming hole between Goldie's Mill and Gow's Bridge on the Speed River, ever watchful for police chief Jonathan Kelly, who made it his mission to discourage such delinquency. They were all terrified of Kelly.

If it was a particularly hot summer day, he'd catch up with the horse-drawn Halliburton's ice wagon as it made its rounds, and the driver would give him some ice chips. To Arthur's way of thinking, it was the best treat in the world.

In winters, he went tobogganing on the Macdonald farm, rocketing down the hills, through the swirling snow devils, hollering with joy. Hours he'd stay, until his fingers and toes were frozen, and his eyebrows were frosted white.

He was an ace at marbles, winning a huge collection from his schoolmates and displaying his spoils in a box with a glass top. "Cutten became a skillful player and soon gathered to himself a great treasure of marbles. These were of all varieties, but what Cutten desired was the more expensive marbles known as glassies," *Maclean's* magazine later reported. "Finally, there came a morning when his chums could dig up no more glassies ... The boy who was to grow up to be a dictator of the wheat pit had successfully cornered every glassie in the school."[7]

But Arthur's true passion was baseball. Whenever his hometown heroes the Guelph Maple Leafs were battling it out with visiting rivals, he scampered out to the exhibition grounds to watch and cheer his beloved team. When local pitcher Fred Dyson broke into the professional leagues playing for the Grand Rapids and Buffalo clubs,[8] Arthur dreamed that someday he too could become a pro player in the US, "where such glorious creatures were properly esteemed."[9]

And if he didn't make it in baseball, well then, he would settle for becoming the driver of the Wellington Hotel's omnibus.

His siblings and friends – among them Charlie Dunbar, Robert Torrance, and Herb Leadley – all called him "Buzz." The nickname came about when a younger member of Arthur's family kept referring to him as "buzzer": the little tyke had a lisp and couldn't pronounce "brother." The moniker stuck.[10]

On 23 April 1879, Guelph achieved city status. Although it was slightly short of the ten thousand in population needed to become a city, the provincial government passed an act conferring the title on Guelph in recognition of its fifty-second anniversary. It was a day of great jubilation. Stores, buildings, and residences were festooned with flags and bunting. A gala parade was organized, the largest in the history of the community, one that took twenty-two minutes to pass a single point along the route.

Arthur Cutten and his pals watched as the marching bands and horse-drawn wagons wound by. At the head of the parade was Thomas Lynch, the first male born in the old settlement, followed by the mayor and aldermen. Next came the fire brigades with their shiny water pumps, members of the local militia marching in step, pipers and drummers, and the decorated floats.

Sitting atop a monster cask of Sleeman's beer was 350-pound Walter Cook. That got a good laugh from the crowd. Then there was John Bunyan and his ox cart, a working loom sponsored by J. & A. Armstrong's Carpet, a Bell organ being played in thunderous peals, Myer's Prime Cigars handing out samples, and confectioner Weir Bryce & Co. tossing sweets to the children. "Buzz" and his gang followed,

Arthur "Buzz" Cutten at age ten. A shy and socially awkward kid, but an ace at marbles and math.

*The Sunset home on Paisley Street in Guelph, built in 1874 for
Walter Hoyt Cutten. The family lived here until 1889 when Walter had to sell
the property because of financial losses.*

dodging and weaving through the throngs, snagging as many candies
as they could.

Arthur's father, Walter, was an important lawyer in town. Walter had
graduated from Osgoode Hall in Toronto and had been admitted to the
bar in 1867.[11] One year later, he married Annie MacFadden of London,
Ontario. They settled in Guelph where they rented a stone cottage.
A few years later, they built their own home, a two-storey limestone
house known as Sunset, which still stands today on Paisley Street.

Guelph was then enjoying a period of prosperity. After the Grand
Trunk Railway reached it from Toronto in 1856, the dusty little village had begun to grow. Alongside the traditional breweries, found-
ries, flour mills, and lumber dealers, newly established manufacturing
operations such as the Raymond Sewing Machine Company and the

Bell Organ Company were expanding rapidly and even exporting internationally.

Spacious homes and handsome shops sprouted up. Well-appointed hotels were constructed. Women had the latest fashions. Men smoked cigars and sipped good whisky in their clubs.

Walter became a partner in a prominent local law firm (Guthrie, Watt and Cutten), and in quick succession he and Annie had children: Edward (born 1869), Arthur (1870), Lionel (1872), Mary (1873, died in infancy), Lenore (1874), Harry (1876), Charles (1877), Constance (1879), and Ralph (1883). With this expanding brood, two live-in maids were needed, and Annie Murphy and Mary Cushin were added to the household.[12]

The Cuttens lived in relative affluence. Walter's practice was successful, they moved in the right social circles, and the family attended every Sunday at St George's Church. They were a model of respectability. They were, after all, thoroughly British.

Peering through the mists of history, we can find the Cutten ancestors (then named "Cutting") living near Ardleigh, in the county of Essex, England, in the early sixteenth century. Generations farmed and were laid to rest there, until this quiet existence was disrupted by a deep economic depression as well as by political and religious upheaval. After King Charles I dissolved Parliament in 1629, a wave of emigration ensued. Over the next decade, more than eighty thousand men, women, and children left England, with about twenty thousand settling in the Massachusetts Bay area.

Caught up in this exodus was a boy of eleven, Richard Cutting, who sailed from Ipswitch on the *Elizabeth* in April 1634.[13] Along with his mother Susan and stepfather Henry Kemball and some one hundred other passengers, the lad reached Boston after a voyage of about nine weeks. The family put down roots in Watertown, and for the next 125 years their descendants lived and prospered in the region.

But by the mid-1700s, there was little cheap land still available in the more established colonies, and the younger men were having to look further afield to homestead. Again, economic and political forces conspired to drive the Cuttens to greener pastures.

Up in the colony of Nova Scotia, Governor Charles Lawrence was offering land grants. The British had defeated the French and expelled most of the Acadian (Roman Catholic) population, and an influx of (Protestant) farmers was urgently needed. One group from Massachusetts Bay to apply included David Cutting, and in 1760 he was among the settlers to sail into the Bay of Fundy and take up land at Cobequid (later Onslow Township).

This was the first wave of the New England Planters, roughly two thousand families from the lower colonies that were attracted to the area by the offer of good farmland. They became known as the Bluenosers to distinguish them from the later settlers, the United Empire Loyalists, who left the American colonies after the War of Independence.

David Cutting/Cutten (this is when the surname seems to have been modified) was elected in 1761 as one of the first two members to represent Onslow Township in the Nova Scotia General Assembly. His descendants spoke of his having walked on snow shoes, carrying a musket on his shoulder, to attend the winter session in Halifax. (The official records show only that he won in a by-election on 7 September 1761 but never sat in the Assembly.[14])

The next push westward occurred when Edward Logan Cutten (David's great-grandson) made his way to Upper Canada. In 1841, he and Jemima Lowell were married in the Bayham First Baptist Church,[15] and they took up farming in the Haysville area.[16] Over a dozen years they had six children. Edward Logan was a shrewd businessman, and in addition to his agricultural pursuits, he operated a number of hotels at various times, including the Queen's Arms Hotel in Galt,[17] Cutten House in Strathroy,[18] and Strong's Hotel in London.[19]

For the first time, the Cuttens were no longer entirely dependent on the land for a living. Edward Logan was well enough off to send his eldest son, Walter Hoyt Cutten, to law school in Toronto. Think of that. It was now possible to reach beyond the grasp of one's forefathers. It was an extraordinary development – one that reflected the shifting social and economic dynamics of this new country called Canada.

In 1882, lawyer Walter set up a private banking business. He purchased the Guelph Banking Company from Augustus T. Kerr and became its sole shareholder. He resigned his partnership with Guthrie and Watt, but continued to practise law independently while carrying on his financing operations.

In those days, private banks were owned by local businessmen who simply rented an office, hung out a sign, and began taking deposits and writing loans.[20] Private banks were completely unregulated, meaning they operated free of any audit, inspection, reporting, security, or reserve requirements.

Cutten's operation was supported by the chartered Federal Bank, which loaned money to a network of private banks in the smaller towns of southwestern Ontario in addition to running its own branches. Chartered banks liked this arrangement because it allowed them to get around the provisions of the Bank Act and, through such networks, expand their lending into areas they were prohibited from serving directly.

The Guelph Banking Company loaned money to less creditworthy farms and businesses, charging a higher rate of interest, and then used these notes as collateral to obtain loans from Federal. To attract depositors, Cutten offered two points above the standard rate. The local newspaper observed that, "as Mr. Cutten was a keen financier and lawyer, he doubtless ran risks and made money where more conservative men would not."[21]

Thinking big now, Walter wanted new premises that would reflect the growing success of his bank. He purchased a property at the corner of Wyndham and Macdonell Streets (jointly financed with local pharmacist Alexander B. Petrie) and commissioned the construction of what became known as the Petrie-Cutten Block. Designed by architect John Day, the building was completed in 1883, and the Guelph Banking Company opened its office.

People trusted Walter Cutten, and the bank prospered. As one farmer put it, he had every confidence in the young man because he "was paying 6 per cent, and besides, with such a fine block (building location) and a fast horse, I thought he was perfectly safe!"[22]

By 1883, Walter Hoyt Cutten had so improved his station that it was fitting for his two eldest boys to attend Trinity College School. Located on a hilltop in Port Hope (east of Toronto), TCS had been founded eighteen years earlier by Anglican minister Father William Johnson. The private institution, modelled on the boarding schools of

Arthur's high school, the Guelph Collegiate Institute.

England, was much favoured by the wealthy for the proper training
and education of their male heirs. And so it was that Arthur and his
older brother Edward were accepted into "the school on the hill," arriving with their trunks in September.

The year passed in a rather unremarkable way. Reverend Charles
Bethune was the headmaster. The only records remaining at TCS
note that the Cutten boys were confirmed in the Anglican Church
on 6 April 1884 and that they departed for summer holidays on 1 July.
Arthur would only recall that they played cricket, "but God save the
Queen, we preferred baseball."[23] Much to their relief, they were returned to the public school system the following academic year.

After completing his formal education, Arthur spent a few "lost
years" trying to figure out what he wanted to do with his life. The
economy was depressed and employment was difficult to find. He remembered "lounging about my father's offices on the theory that I
was working and eventually might read law."[24] He imagined that, like
so many other young men of his generation, he would leave for the
US, where jobs were more plentiful.

He worked for a brief stint at the US Consulate in Guelph. He filled
out certificates and performed other minor duties under the supervision of Consul James W. Childs, earning four dollars a week and enjoying the fact that the US government officially employed him (if only
for six months).

Arthur Cutten, about twenty years of age, with sisters and friends in Guelph. Back row left to right: Hila Loscombe, Arthur Cutten, Connie Cutten, George Morris. Front row left to right: Dr Coglin, Alice Higinbotham, Lenore Cutten.

He applied at local businesses, thinking his facility with numbers would be an asset, but none were hiring. He grew restless and frustrated, and felt he was "getting old."

When he had nothing else to do, Arthur would trek six or seven miles out of Guelph to visit a black-whiskered farmer named Alexander Hill. Alex would keep him spellbound with stories about his famous brother, James Jerome Hill, who had left Canada for the US, where he was building a vast railway empire that would become the Great Northern line. "I worked out for myself the notion that the essential difference between the brothers was that one had stayed home and one had gone out into the world," said Cutten. "I think that this was what settled the matter for me."[25]

But perhaps there was another reason for wanting to leave Guelph, something that Arthur never mentioned publicly.

On 30 January 1888, a notice was posted on the doors of the Guelph Banking Company. It read: *Owing to the winding up of the Federal Bank, and heavy losses sustained, the Guelph Banking Company is obliged to suspend for the present and go into liquidation, particulars whereof will be made*

known in due time to parties interested. Arthur's father, Walter Hoyt, had
gone bust.

The Federal Bank, unable to meet its own obligations, demanded
the repayment of its loans to Cutten, which, in turn, triggered the
failure of the Guelph Banking Company. According to the rumours,
Cutten owed about $20,000 to the Federal, $25,000 to depositors, and
some $40,000 to four wealthy individuals who had provided loans to
his bank – a total of $85,000, which is equivalent to more than $2 million today.

In a desperate effort to stay afloat, Cutten had gone deeply into
debt. He had made a series of disastrous investments with Augustus
T. Kerr, who, after selling him the bank, had set up a brokerage firm in
Toronto. The *New York Times* reported that the cause of the collapse
was Cutten's transactions with bucket shops.[26]

Stephen Thorning, in *Hayseed Capitalists: Private Bankers in Ontario*,
concluded that, "although the Guelph Banking Company was one of
the many private banks to try to sustain a business on shaky borrow-
ers and naïve depositors, it still might have survived had it not been
for W.H. Cutten's unwise real estate investments and stock specula-
tions."[27] The news was on everyone's lips. The local *Guelph Daily Mercury and Advertise*r reported: "it is understood that Mr. Cutten's real
estate is heavily mortgaged, which goes to deepen the impression that
by some means he is pretty thoroughly cleaned out."[28]

More shocking still, there were allegations that Walter Cutten had
misappropriated his customers' funds. It was claimed that he received
money from various clients to pay off loans, discharge mortgages, and
invest in properties, and instead he had pocketed the funds for his own
purposes. "In his double capacity of solicitor and banker, he was enabled for a long time to partially satisfy solicitous creditors, even after
there was no hope of retrieving matters," the *Daily Mercury* reported.[29]
"Ultimately, his actions crossed the boundary of legality," Thorning
noted. "He altered cheques and began to put partial payments on loans
into his own pocket."[30]

On 28 February 1888, Cutten was arrested on a charge of obtaining
money on false pretences. At the preliminary hearing, Thomas Caraher, an area farmer, testified that he had paid off a promissory note to
Cutten. But instead of discharging the note, the banker had secretly

*The Guelph Banking Company was located in the building at the right,
corner of Wyndham and Macdonell Streets.*

assigned it as collateral in obtaining a $4,000 loan for himself. The case
was sent to trial court.

Three additional charges were brought by William Kay, a wealthy
retired farmer, who claimed that Cutten had swindled him out of
$5,600 in total. In the first case, Kay said Cutten had asked him for a
$3,000 loan, offering a second mortgage on his house and other real
estate. Kay agreed, but later found that his account had been debited
for $3,500, not $3,000, and that the security was worthless as Cutten's
properties were already fully mortgaged. Kay claimed he also made
payments of $1,500 to a man in Walkerton and $600 to a certain Miss
Leslie of Puslinch – both of which were sent through Cutten but never
reached them. These cases were also assigned to trial.

During one of the hearings, Cutten had difficulty immediately ar-
ranging bail and therefore was to have been held in jail over the weekend. However, as a member of the legal fraternity, it appears he was

given special treatment. An outraged newspaper editor commented: "Instead of spending from Saturday to Monday in Castle Mercer [the Guelph lockup] he enjoyed the privacy of his own home. The public probably don't care much where Mr. Cutten puts in this time, but they are anxious to know how this special privilege was granted to him and on whose authority."[31]

When the four charges of fraud and misappropriation finally went to trial later in the year, everything seemed to go in Cutten's favour.[32] The judge in the Caraher case, feeling the evidence was not clear enough, directed the jury to return a verdict of "not guilty."

In the case of the $3,500 mortgage that Cutten had obtained from Kay, the Crown prosecutor failed to produce any of the documents, and the charge was dismissed. Similarly, in the case of the missing $1,500 that Cutten had been instructed to transfer, the judge "offered a curious ruling that the law did not cover the evidence in such a transaction, and dismissed the case."[33]

And after Miss Leslie failed to appear in court to testify about the $600, the judge instructed the jury to give a verdict of "not guilty" without deliberation. Again, the local newspaper raised questions about the proceedings. The *Mercury* commented: "it seems rather peculiar to the average layman that the crown counsel showed so little interest in the case as not to procure the evidence of Miss Leslie, whose testimony was vital to substantiate the facts."[34]

It appeared that the legal "brotherhood" had closed ranks and kept Cutten out of jail. But while found not guilty in court, Walter Cutten paid a price in the community. His reputation was in tatters, and, in a place such as Guelph, memories were generational. He had to resign his position as an alderman and chairman of the town's Finance Committee. He was forced to sell his share of the downtown office block to his partner Alexander B. Petrie to pay off some of his debts. And within a year, even the family home on Paisley Street was sold.

It was a crushing humiliation for a man who had come so far, so quickly, and prided himself on his social standing.

For Arthur, then, there may have been more to leaving his hometown than dreams of fortune. There may have also been a sense of shame. And a quiet determination to earn back the respect that his father had squandered, to redeem the family name.

Cutten boarded a train from this station, bound for Chicago, in 1890.

And so on 5 May 1890,[35] he climbed aboard a train headed for Chicago. The steam engine belched black smoke as it pulled away from the station. He was nineteen. He had ninety dollars in his pocket.

The train swept through Berlin (now Kitchener) and Stratford and on to Sarnia where it was ferried across the St Clair River and then continued its way westward.

Arthur watched, fascinated, as the towns and cities flashed by – Laperre, Durand, Lansing, Battle Creek, South Bend – the train finally swinging around the southern end of Lake Michigan. In the distance, he could see Chicago, rising out of the smoke. It was monstrous, one hundred times the size of Guelph, sprawling and filthy, and mad in its industry. For the young man, it was love at first sight.

Augustus T. Kerr: Fast Money

AUGUSTUS T. KERR.

Bad boy Augustus T. Kerr.

A.T. Kerr, it turned out, was a con man and fraudster.

Born in 1846 in the small village of Perth, Canada West, Augustus Theophilus was known more commonly as "Gus." His parents, immigrants from Ireland, raised a large family of seven boys and three girls. His father George was a successful merchant in town.[36]

Kerr married Susannah Clement in Ottawa in 1867, and a year later they had a daughter, Millie. He worked as a bank teller in Montreal and then was posted to various branches around Ontario. By the mid-1870s, he was living in Guelph and had become the senior partner in Kerr & MacKellar, a private banking, brokerage, and investment business. This is when he met the young lawyer Walter Hoyt Cutten. Both were ambitious, and both were chasing fast money.

Kerr sold his bank to Cutten and then moved to Toronto where he used the proceeds to become a member of the stock exchange and establish a brokerage firm located at the corner of Scott and Front Streets.[37] Cutten maintained business connections with Kerr and invested with him in a number of highly speculative ventures.[38] Ultimately, this association was one of the factors leading to Walter Hoyt's ruin.

By 1887, Kerr had moved to Buffalo where he was operating another brokerage firm and living with a married woman named Harriet. According to the testimony of her husband, Kerr had "led her astray" with a "profuse display of jewellery and money."[39]

Next, we find him being charged with fraudulently obtaining money from the Central Bank of Toronto.[40] After the Central failed in late 1887, an investigation revealed that certain funds had been diverted to favoured individuals.[41] It was alleged that Kerr had been able to cash worthless cheques at the bank. Narrowly escaping conviction, he left Canada for good.

He surfaced in Kansas City, Missouri, where he worked as a bookkeeper for the Jarvis-Conklin Mortgage Trust Company. His salary was $175 a month, yet he and Harriet resided at the Midland Hotel, the city's finest, and were living far beyond his means. Then in early 1892 he stole $14,000 of negotiable securities from his employer, and the couple vanished.[42]

The American Surety Company, which had issued a bond protecting Jarvis-Conklin against such losses, sent its chief investigator to hunt down the fugitive. Detective J.W. Bowman spent the next six months following the trail, from New York to England, crossing into France, through Germany, Denmark, Norway, and Sweden, to the casinos of Monte Carlo, and back to England, where, with assistance from Scotland Yard, Kerr was finally apprehended.

US secretary of state John Foster made a formal request for extradition, and Kerr, bound in shackles and accompanied by Detective Bowman, found himself on a steamer to New York and thence by train to Kansas City. On 17 March 1893, a jury found him guilty of grand larceny, and he was sentenced to two and half years in Jefferson City penitentiary.[43] He died in Los Angeles in 1920 at the age of seventy-three.

CHAPTER TWO

The Apprentice

Under the smoke, dust all over his mouth, laughing with white teeth,
Under the terrible burden of destiny laughing as a young man laughs,
Laughing even as an ignorant fighter laughs who has never lost a battle,
Bragging and laughing that under his wrist is the pulse,
and under his ribs the heart of the people,
Laughing!

CARL SANDBURG, "CHICAGO"

It was a place of both incredible squalor and sensational wealth. Chicago was the gateway between the vast new agricultural regions and the markets to the east. Almost all of the grain and livestock produced west of the Mississippi River passed through the city. The Union stockyards processed some 9 million animals annually. The slaughterhouses and meatpackers occupied more than a square mile.

Almost 40 per cent of its 1 million residents were first-generation Americans, with thousands upon thousands of immigrants arriving every year from Germany, Ireland, Poland, and Italy. They crowded into slums and poor neighbourhoods. Poverty and disease were commonplace. Women and children worked in sweatshops, and the belching smoke from factories darkened the sky. The Levee area, between Wabash Avenue and Clark Street and from Eighteenth to Twenty-Second Streets, was the heart of the red-light district. Barrooms and gambling dens filled the south side.

At the same time, great fortunes were being made by men like department store magnate Marshall Field, inventor Cyrus McCormick, sleeping car manufacturer George Pullman, retail giants Richard Sears and A.C. Roebuck as well as Aaron Montgomery Ward, and meat

Armour & Company, Union Stock Yards, ca. 1910.

packer P.D. (Philip Danforth) Armour. The multi-millionaires owned mansions on Prairie Avenue, along lower Michigan Avenue, or on Lake Shore Drive. Typically, this was not old money: these were the new rich.

Perhaps there was no better symbol of the divide between rich and poor than the Chicago World's Fair of 1893. Commemorating the four hundredth anniversary of Columbus's arrival in the New World, the exposition encompassed six hundred acres of alabaster buildings along the shores of Lake Michigan. Dubbed the White City, its idyllic parks and neoclassical structures presented a stunning, utopian vision of industrial progress. Visitors walked the grounds in awe of the grandeur and magnificence of what was possible in modern America. While outside the gates, in the dark city, appetite and unrest burned in the belly of the beast.

Arthur Cutten took a room in a boarding house at Dearborn and Ontario Streets on the North Side for six dollars a week. He found work in a hardware store on Lake Street, earning barely more than his rent. A series of menial jobs followed, each lasting only a few weeks or months. He worked as a stock boy in Marshall Field's Wholesale Store, where he quickly came to the conclusion that he "was not designed to be a merchant."[1]

His next stints were as a store salesman at Atwood's Haberdashery and then as a clerk at Charles H. Besley Company (a machinists' supply and copper and brass goods business) where he toiled from 7:00 a.m. to 6:00 p.m. and was so tired after work that he would just go to bed. He moved on to Hately Brothers, packers and provision exporters, where he stayed for a brief time.

His only form of entertainment was playing baseball on Saturday afternoons. He was a member of the Hyde Parks, which went up against other amateur teams, such as the Idlewilds (made up of Northwestern University students) and Douglaston. To Arthur's chagrin, some of the clubs started bringing in professional players, which spoiled the competition and led to the breakup of the league.

After more than a year, Arthur was having a pretty dull time of it. But he had learned an important lesson. "I had discovered that the acquisition of capital, much more than luck, was apt to govern the fate of a man trying to advance himself from obscurity."[2]

Then, in July 1891, he landed a position that would change his life. It was with A. Stamford White & Co., a stock, bond, and commodities brokerage house that also specialized in buying meats for export to England, France, Germany, and other countries. His boss, whose name the company bore, was a portly, whiskered gentleman and a fixture on the exchange.

Arthur was hired as a bookkeeper and clerk. As part of his job, he was required to go to the exchange floor in the mornings to obtain the opening prices of grains and other commodities. On his first visit, he was awestruck. Men crowded around the trading pits where they bought and sold, using hand signals and barking their orders, closing deals worth hundreds of thousands of dollars without anything written down, a great hubbub of excitement and commotion where fortunes were lost and won. "Neither baseball careers nor bugle calls nor anything else had so much power to stir my mind and emotions," he exclaimed.[3]

Whenever he could, Cutten hung out in the Pigeon Roost, a small area above the pits, where he could study the action. There on the exchange floor, sitting in a chair tilted back against a pillar, was Jim Patten himself. He was chewing gum, as usual, his big red mustache moving in a wide arc. The Cudahy brothers were circling the provision pit, ready to sell millions of pounds of meat if the price was right. William Bartlett and Frank Frazier, their eyes riveted on wheat prices, conferred with Patten as they plotted their next campaign.

Cutten often ate at Kohlsaat's restaurant in the old Royal Insurance Building. It was one of the first lunch counters in Chicago where customers sat on stools and were served sandwiches and other quick-service foods, their hats still on their heads, crowded elbow to elbow. On one occasion, he found himself sitting next to Benjamin P. Hutchinson.

"Old Hutch" was famous among the traders and dealers for having once been the shrewdest operator on the Chicago Board of Trade (CBOT). Back in the spring of 1888 he engineered a corner in wheat. He began purchasing futures contracts at around eighty-six cents a bushel. Prices slowly rose through the summer as he bought up the supply. Edwin Pardridge, his old nemesis in the pits, was shorting – selling contracts in the belief that wheat was headed lower and that he would be able to cover his position at depressed prices and make a profit on the difference. And then an early frost swept over the Red River Valley destroying a large part of the crop, and by September wheat was at two dollars. "Old Hutch" made millions.

Cutten had heard the stories about this legendary speculator – how he had started as a shoe and boot manufacturer in Massachusetts, moved to Chicago where he grew wealthy by suppling meat to the Union Army during the Civil War, and established the Chicago Packing and Provision Company as well as the Corn Exchange Bank.[4]

Without a word passing between them, Cutten watched in fascination as this tall, thin man slurped at his soup. Hutchinson was dressed in clothes that had been fashionable at the time of Abraham Lincoln some thirty years earlier. His coat was buttoned at the top, and his doeskin pants did not reach his ankle bones. Beneath the wide brim of a black slouch hat, his fierce eyes and hawk nose gave him the look of a predator. And then "Old Hutch" was gone, like an apparition, disappearing into the afternoon.

Benjamin Hutchinson.

With his new job at A.S. White & Co., Cutten was now able to afford slightly better accommodation, sharing a room in a big house. The residence, located near Congress Street and Michigan Avenue, even had electric light. The rent was forty dollars a month.

The young apprentice was learning the intricacies of trading in commodities. One of his first observations about the pits was that the loudest voices were not always the most successful traders. Secrecy was crucial to putting together a big operation. He discovered that those who truly played the grain markets well were serious students of weather patterns, insect infestations, world supply and demand figures, and a host of other factors. He watched the great ones and found that they bought and sold based on the information they had acquired, not on the tips and gossip proffered by others. They cut their losses quickly but allowed their gains to mount.

These were lessons he would apply throughout his career. It was an education that he could have had nowhere else. He was learning from the masters, and Cutten was an astute observer of human nature. He recognized that it was greed and fear that fuelled the markets, and he saw that both the irrational gains driven by dreams of easy money and the terrifying plunges induced by panic were golden opportunities for those few who could control their emotions and trade with the quiet confidence of their convictions.

He revered the big players, they were his heroes and his role models. If you could survive by your wits, if you could outmanoeuvre your opponents and beat them at the game, that was success. There was no room for sympathy. There was only the score.

It took five years, but finally Arthur persuaded his boss that he was ready to work as a full-time broker in the pits. On 11 November 1896, Cutten became a member of the Chicago Board of Trade. A. Stamford White gave him an eight-hundred-dollar loan to cover his membership cost.

He would be buying and selling commodities on behalf of clients, and his starting salary would be $150 a month. As well, the firm would permit him to scalp for himself – make short-term trades on small price movements in corn, wheat, rye, barley, and oats in order to supplement his wages.

Cutten arrived that morning, stopped outside the Board of Trade building, and caught his breath. He looked up at the massive structure, constructed of steel and granite, Chicago's tallest at the time. Two large statues, one representing Agriculture and the other Industry, stared down from the capstone above the main entrance. He stepped inside and entered the eighty-foot-high great hall that was decorated by a stained-glass skylight and massive marble columns.

He received his first order and nervously walked out onto the exchange floor. He was twenty-six. With his thin mustache, starched shirt, and new trading jacket, he looked like the rookie he was. The

Chicago Board of Trade, 1900. Above the main entrance are the statues representing Agriculture and Industry.

Board of Trade during session, ca. 1905.

veteran traders gave him the once over and then turned back to their business as though he was of no consequence.

Cutten moved purposely to the corn pit and, in the open-outcry method, shouted out an order to buy one hundred September corn (100,000 bushels for delivery in September). He took twenty-five thousand bushels from each of four men and the order was filled. "I was exalted. This was, for me, a kind of knighthood."[5] He would add later: "The day I first walked onto the floor of the exchange as a member was a scarlet one for me; and no wonder for it was in the pits that I learned how to make money."

Cutten learned how to trade on margin (putting up only a portion of the cost to increase his potential returns) and to buy and sell for fractions of a cent. He became skilful in moving from long positions (buying securities with the expectation that they would increase in value) to short positions (borrowing securities and selling them, hoping to buy them back later at a lower price) and back again in minutes. He rarely traded more than ten thousand bushels at a time but made twenty to thirty trades a day. The money was good, but he knew that he was never going to get really rich. Scalping, by its nature, was short term, and he'd never be able to catch the big swings. He wanted more than a comfortable living. He wanted to make a killing.

Arthur's brother Charley had joined him in Chicago, and the two were now boarding with Edson and Bill White, twin brothers from Peoria. They roomed in a pretentious red-brick house on Grand Boulevard, just south of Forty-First Street. Tom Wilson, a young man from London, Ontario, whose family had immigrated some years earlier, was a frequent visitor and close friend.[6]

The Whites were employed at Armour & Company, and both would go on to top positions in the meat-packing company – Edson as president and Bill as vice-president. Wilson was also working his way up in the same industry at Morris & Co. and later would become president of Wilson & Company, the third largest meat packers in the US.

Charley, too, had a similar job at Continental Packing Company. More than six feet tall, Charley was the biggest lad in the Cutten family. He was eager, bold, full of laughter and boisterousness, and, like "Buzz," he was here to make his mark in this hog-butchering city.

Among his chums, Arthur was considered the oddity. While they attended theatres, splurged on sixty-dollar suits, and pursued young women, "Cutten seldom took in any amusements, making the excuse that he didn't have the money to spend," *Maclean's* magazine reported: "They could never quite fathom or understand Cutten. He always seemed a man apart."[7] Cutten himself acknowledged his social awkwardness. "I never was much of a hand to mix. I think I was a little shy in company."[8]

On Christmas Day 1898, Arthur attended a dinner at the home of his boss. Returning to the boarding house later that evening, he had a broad smile on his face and a cheque for five hundred dollars in his hand.

"I found it under my plate," said Cutten. "A Christmas gift from the old man."

Frank Edson White, one of Cutten's friends and roommates
when he first arrived in Chicago.

Bill White whistled in amazement.

"I've had a pretty good year. With this, plus my $1,800 salary and my scalping, I've made more than $4,000." Cutten was now earning almost as much from speculating as he was from trading for others.

One night, Charley came home from work with a bandaged forearm. The boys knew immediately what had happened, and they inquired as to the seriousness of the injury.

*Thomas Wilson, fellow Canadian and another of
Cutten's early friends in Chicago.*

"Aw, it's nothing much, not more than a scratch," laughed Charley. It went with the job. As did the bravado.

As part of his training, the twenty-two-year-old had been learning the various cuts of meat. The knife had slipped and sliced into his arm.

They thought nothing of it. They didn't know that the knife had been tainted by the blood of a tubercular pig. Within months, Charley had become dreadfully thin, and there were bright scarlet patches on his cheeks. He packed his bags for home.

Arthur was shattered.

They stood on the station platform, Arthur and the White boys, bidding their friend and brother goodbye. As the train pulled out, there were quiet tears. Soon thereafter, Charley died in Guelph. One of them had been lost.

Laconically, years later, Arthur Cutten would observe: "All the youngsters who came to Chicago to seek their fortune did not find what they came for."[9]

Edson White married a Canadian, Lillian Pearson, in 1899. His brother Bill was best man and Cutten was an usher at the wedding held at the Maple Street Methodist Church in her hometown of Collingwood, Ontario.[10] The boys were surprised and delighted when the head of Armour & Company put his private railway car at their disposal so they could travel in grand style to the small town north of Toronto, and apparently this caused quite a sensation.[11]

Tom Wilson was also married that same year to Elizabeth "Lizzie" Foss of Chicago.

Arthur, bashful and introverted, especially around women, took a few more years to tie the knot. In any event, he would have told you, he was much too busy learning how to turn grain into money.

The old was making way for the new. Great changes were around the corner. The Spanish-American War had launched the US into world affairs, and the country was entering a long period of rapid growth. Technological innovation was about to deliver airplanes, motion pictures, and mass-produced cars. Returning a war hero from his service with the Rough Riders in Cuba, Teddy Roosevelt would become president upon McKinley's assassination. Soon, work on the Panama Canal would get under way.

Increasingly, industrial capital was falling into fewer and fewer hands. United States Steel Corporation would be the first billion-dollar company. At the same time, unions were organizing and gaining power. People were migrating to urban centres and jobs. Within two decades, there would be more US citizens living in cities than on farms and in small towns.

And at the close of the nineteenth century, "Old Hutch" was losing money in a series of disastrous plays. Leaving Chicago, he drifted around New England for a time and then turned up in New York where he was spending his last dollars on the Produce Exchange. His family placed him in a sanitarium in Lake Geneva, Wisconsin, where he died in 1899.

James Patten now gained prominence as king of the trading pits, launching a series of successful campaigns over the next decade. He drove the price of oats from thirty-four cents to sixty-five cents a bushel. He took $2 million out of the corn market. In 1909, he engineered what became known as the "Patten Corner" in wheat, walking away with more than $4 million for himself and his associates.[12] His moves were coldly calculated and boldly executed, and were much admired by Cutten.

Arthur was making some money in corn and was also dabbling in the stock market. In 1904 he took a flyer on the Soo Line railroad, purchasing two thousand shares at fifty-four dollars a share and selling two years later at $164, pocketing $220,000. Small change compared to what his trades would yield in the future, but still a tidy profit. "This was my real start," he recalled. It also confirmed his notion that he'd never make serious money trading for others. "It would have been foolish for me to continue working as a pit broker after the culmination of that Soo Line deal. So I resigned."[13]

Characteristically, Cutten simply did not show up for work the next day. Shortly after the market opened, A. Stamford White found him on the trading floor. "What the blazes are you doing, Arthur?" he demanded.

"Oh, I forgot to tell you, I'm on my own now," Cutten replied.[14]

It was a pivotal moment in his career, and, although nervous, he was also elated. He had a decade of experience in the pits, and he felt he had reached the point at which he had to decide: Would he live a secure, middling life as a customer's man or would he trust his own talents and put everything on the line?

Arthur really had little choice. The image of his father, broken and disgraced, was always in his mind. The apprenticeship was over. He was ready to launch himself on one of the most spectacular trajectories ever witnessed in the markets.

By 1905, Arthur was doing well enough that he was able to purchase a fine house in Guelph as a gift for his family. Located on Stuart Street,

Tranquille on Stuart Street, Guelph. Arthur Cutten
purchased this house in 1905.

the property was called Tranquille. His father and mother moved in, as
did some of his brothers and sisters, and it remained in the family for
many years. Arthur would stay at Tranquille whenever he visited his
hometown. The yellow brick home with its distinctive two-storey ve-
randah was one of the most beautiful residences in the city, and ownership of the property restored some of the lustre to the Cutten name.

Finally, Arthur met Miss Maud Boomer. She lived in Evanston with
her mother Martha, brother Paul, and sisters Agnes and Permelia. Her
father Norton, who had died years earlier, had been the principal of
the Franklin School in North Evanston.[15]

Maud had worked for a time as a "saleslady" in various high-end
women's fashion shops in Chicago, including the Alaska Fur Co. on
State Street, and milliners Louise & Co. on Michigan Avenue.[16] She

Arthur's wife, Maud (Boomer) Cutten.

was five feet and five inches tall and had short brown hair, blue eyes, and a round face.[17] Like Arthur, she was shy and retiring, and although she attended various society functions, she preferred the quiet of home. They were immediately attracted to one another.

On Saturday, 12 May 1906, Arthur and Maud were married in the Trinity Episcopal Church in Highland Park, north of Chicago. The marriage licence records his age as thirty-five, hers as thirty (there are many conflicting records as to her birthdate). The newlyweds moved into a swanky apartment at the Chicago Beach Hotel.

A. Stamford White: Gave Cutten His Start

*A. Stamford White, the man who gave
Cutten his first job in the grain pits.*

Alfred Stamford White was impressed enough by the young
Canadian to offer him a position with his Chicago brokerage
and provisions export firm. Cutten's facility for numbers, his
attention to detail, and his earnest desire to learn were just the
qualities that White wanted in a junior employee. Arthur was
hired as a clerk and bookkeeper in July 1891. Neither could
have known that this small step was the beginning of one of
the most spectacular careers in the history of the markets.

In fact, while White considered Cutten well suited to work
in his shop, he cautioned the budding speculator not to set
his sights too high. "You are a smart young man, Arthur. You

must know that a man of modest means cannot trade in the commodities market. It would be sheer lunacy ... You heed my advice and you will thank me for it later. My advice is to avoid the commodities market, avoid the stock market."[18] Cutten, obviously, ignored the admonition.

White was born in the city of Liverpool, England, in 1851. He completed high school and then started in the grain and provisions business. In 1881 he came to the US and established operations in Chicago. He joined the CBOT and rapidly built a successful transatlantic enterprise. He married Florence Broomhall, and by 1900 they were living with their three children, along with a housekeeper, cook, and coachman, in a grand residence on Lexington Avenue.[19]

White served twice as president of the CBOT, in 1910 and 1918, respectively. He was an early supporter of the Boy Scouts of America and was instrumental in establishing the Owasippe Scout Reservation in Twin Lake, Michigan, the first scout camp in the United States. He was a member of the board of managers of the Chicago YMCA, a trustee for the Chicago Home for Boys, and a director of Quaker Oats Co. and the Chicago Savings Bank and Trust Co.

During the war, he worked with Herbert Hoover's US Food Administration in its efforts to conserve food supplies at home and help feed America's allies. In 1918, shortly after returning from one of his trips to Washington, DC, he fell ill and died from Spanish influenza. The presidency of the CBOT, which he held at the time of his death, was temporarily filled by James Patten (see chapter 3).

Tom Wilson and Edson White: Young Turks

When he first arrived in Chicago, Arthur Cutten met two young men who – like him – were fired with dreams of achieving great things. And they remained pals, getting together later in life to "recount the struggles and adventures of those days when any of them was happy to have made something over and above what paid their board and expenses for the week."[20]

Tom Wilson was an imposing figure – six feet tall, blue-eyed, broad-shouldered, lantern-jawed.[21] He mixed easily and had a wide circle of friends. As he progressed in his career, he was always admired and respected as much by the men and women who worked for him as by the city's business elite. Like Cutten, he became very rich. But he did it by building great businesses.

Born in 1868, Tom was one of eight children raised on a farm near London, Ontario.[22] His father Moses Wilson also had an interest in a small oil refinery in London East. Oil had been discovered in the area twenty years earlier, and this had resulted in a boom. But by 1876, overproduction and liberal free-trade policies with the US had saturated the market and prices fell. Some of the smaller refineries went out of business, others had to consolidate to survive.[23] The Wilson refinery was merged into the Mutual Oil Refining Company of London in 1878 (Mutual itself was absorbed by Imperial Oil Company in 1880).[24]

According to accounts, Moses made a "moderate fortune" in the oil business, enough to move his family to Chicago. Unfortunately, he then met with "financial reverses" that prevented him from sending Tom to college.[25]

At eighteen, Tom was working as a junior clerk for the Chicago, Burlington and Quincy Railroad. By the time he met Cutten a year later, he had landed a forty-dollar-a-month job as car checker (checking incoming loads of livestock) for the meat-packing firm of Morris & Co. Despite the unpleasantness of the stockyards, his determination was evident even then:

"When you got there, you found the plank roads floating in mud which had a knack of squirting up the legs of your pants when you stepped from one plank to another. Everything was rough and crude and uninviting," he recounted. "But there was no lack of business. It looked as if a fellow could find a lot to do. I thought I could see an opportunity for any one willing to work and to stay by the proposition."[26]

He spent the next twenty-five years working his way up. In 1899, he married Elizabeth Foss and they moved into a house on Calumet Avenue. Two children followed soon – Helen in 1900 and Edward in 1905.[27]

When Edward Morris, the founder of Morris & Co., died in 1913, Tom was named president of the firm. Three years later, a banking consortium, which had taken over the failing meat-packing company Sulzberger & Sons, lured Tom away to run the firm. The firm was renamed Wilson & Co. and he became president. He rapidly expanded the company, building it into the third largest meat packer (behind Armour & Swift) and one of the fifty largest industrial corporations in the United States. A visionary and brilliant marketer, he developed many popular value-added beef and pork products.

He also took charge of Ashland Manufacturing Company, a subsidiary of Sulzberger, which had been incorporated in 1913 to produce various goods, including sports equipment, using by-products from the packing operations. For example, it made baseball gloves from cowhide and tennis strings from animal gut. The business, later named Wilson Sporting Goods, would become one of the best-known sporting goods manufacturers in the world. Even a volleyball named Wilson would later star with Tom Hanks in the 2000 movie *Cast Away*.

By the 1920s, the Wilsons were living on Woodlawn Avenue in the Kenwood neighbourhood.[28] Tom also owned a large farm near Lake Forest, named Edellyn, where he raised prize-winning cattle.

Tom and Arthur would visit each other at their country estates where they'd go horseback riding and, over dinner, reminisce about the "good old days."[29] They also played golf together, and both enjoyed the thoroughbred races at Arlington.

Tom retired in 1953. He died on 4 August 1958 (aged ninety) at his farm and was buried at Lake Forest Cemetery, in Lake County, Illinois.

When F. Edson White was appointed president of Armour & Company at the age of forty-nine, he was described in the press as a self-made man, the sort of fellow who demonstrated that, through hard work and perseverance, all things were possible in America. "A man who started in the slime of 'Packingtown' and climbed to the top of the ladder," said the *New York Times*.[30] *Boys' Life: The Boy Scouts' Magazine* urged its young readers to follow in the footsteps of such men as White, who "prove America to be the land of opportunity."[31]

But Edson and his twin brother Bill, born in Peoria, Illinois, on 9 September 1873, did not come from an impoverished background. Their father was a cattle dealer, head of F.C. White & Co., and a prominent member of the city's business community. Through his connections, the boys got jobs in the meat-packing industry; yes, starting out in low positions, but advancing quickly.

Edson attended the public schools until he was seventeen, when he began his career as a travelling salesman for E. Gobel and Sons, a packing company in Peoria. He worked for a couple of years in San Francisco for the Western Meat Company and then went to Chicago, where he was employed by Armour & Company in the car route sales department. By the time he and his brother were living with Arthur and Charley Cutten in a boarding house on Grand Boulevard, Edson had moved up to be manager of the sheep and wool department.[32]

His natural talents for business administration marked him for rapid promotion within the Armour organization. Like his friend Tom Wilson, he was a tall, handsome man with an engaging personality. Edson married Lillian Pearson of Collingwood, Ontario, on 19 October 1899, and they had three children, Gertrude, Georgina, and Frank Jr.

During the First World War, Edson was in charge of meat sales to the US government and the Allied nations.[33] The company ramped up production and experienced massive growth with annual revenue reaching $1 billion. Like his friends Cutten and Wilson, he built a rural estate called White House Farm near Lake Forest.

After the Armistice, demand for the company's products just as quickly declined as government contracts were cancelled, and Armour found itself over-extended, holding huge inventories at lower and lower prices. The company lost $125 million between 1919 and 1921. J. Ogden Amour, president, saw his family fortune bleed away, and at one point he was losing a million dollars a day. "I lost money so fast," J. Ogden said to a friend, "I didn't think it was possible."[34] Unable to reinvigorate the company, he turned over the reins to Edson in 1923.

Within months of assuming the presidency, Edson suffered a terrible blow. His only son, Frank Jr, accidentally shot himself while wielding his gun as a club to ward off a charging bull on the White House Farm.[35]

Through the 1920s, Edson restored the company's profitability, and, under his leadership, it grew to 60,000 employees, 500 branch houses, and 20 packing plants. He was regarded as one of the ablest executives in the packing industry.[36] The Whites divided their time between their country estate and their city apartment on Scott Street.

At fifty-seven, when Edson was at the top of his professional career, tragedy struck again. On the evening of 15 January 1931 – well into the Great Depression – he fell from the bedroom window of his seventh-floor apartment on Scott Street and died instantly from multiple fractures of the skull.[37] He had been sitting on a bench seat in front of an open bay window and apparently had leaned back and toppled out. His death was ruled accidental.[38]

CHAPTER THREE

Of Foe and Friend

Located at East Hyde Park Boulevard, the Chicago Beach Hotel was one of the city's largest and first resorts serving both residential and short-term guests. Built in 1890 at a cost of $1 million, the six-storey hotel featured a one-thousand-foot veranda overlooking the lake and park. Tennis courts, boardwalks, and cabanas dotted the beautiful grounds. Its restaurants were renowned, and the entertainment was first-class. It was the place to be for many wealthy Chicagoans.

For Maud, the hotel apartment was perfect as it was close to the shopping and theatre districts. Arthur liked its open spaces. He had spent too many years living in cramped quarters. Here he could spread out a bit.

From his study, he watched the breakers roll onto the sandy white beach. It was autumn, and the bathers and the cabanas were long gone. Just a lingering sun that lulled everyone with its false promises, even as it dipped lower in the southern sky.

When Arthur arrived home after work, Maud was always able to sense how his day had gone at the Board of Trade. She could read him as easily as he could read a ticker tape. If he appeared with a ready greeting, things were good. If he slapped down his newspaper and hat, the markets were against him.

But he never discussed his deals with her. "Why should I force her to carry such a burden of care? A prize fighter might as fairly expect his wife to share the blows he takes in the ring. The blows a speculator takes when he loses are hard jolts to his nervous system," Cutten explained.[1]

And so, in late October 1907, the emphatic whack of newspaper and hat on the vestibule table left little room for doubt.

Chicago Beach Hotel, 1905.

Cutten had purchased futures contracts for about 6 million bushels of wheat, and the price had been moving in his favour. He had placed this bet on reports of a greenbug outbreak in the Midwest and his study of weather maps, which convinced him that a serious infestation was likely. He had calculated that prices would rise as the crop came in short that year.

Wheat rose, crossing the one-dollar-a-bushel mark.

But then a financial crisis rocked the country. There were bank failures, a loss of public confidence with depositors rushing to withdraw their funds, and a severe contraction of credit on Wall Street. Without access to call loans, brokerage houses were forced to sell stocks to cover margin accounts. Prices plummeted, and the panic spilled onto the grain exchanges as traders began dumping their futures contracts. Wheat slumped to below ninety cents a bushel.

Arthur Cutten in 1908.

"I helplessly watched paper profits evaporate," Cutten remarked. "It does not matter if they are paper when you lose them. When you lose, you sweat blood."[2]

More than seven hundred miles away in New York, Jesse Lauriston (J.L.) Livermore was jubilant. On 24 October, he had plunged into the market, short selling the major stocks and pyramiding his position as prices continued to slide. At the end of trading that day, he tallied up his paper profits. He had made more than $1 million in that single session.

According to Livermore, in a story he loved to recount, he was studying his next move, how he might hammer the market again the following morning, when word came through an intermediary that John Pierpont (J.P.) Morgan was asking him to stop short selling. Morgan and a group of bankers in New York were working to halt the crisis by propping up the system with cash, and Livermore's bear operations would have been detrimental to their efforts.

Livermore claimed that he acceded to this request, and the next day covered his positions and started to buy aggressively as prices rebounded from their lows. Reportedly, he earned another $2 million on the rally. With his winnings, he and his first wife, Nettie Jordan, moved into a beautiful apartment on Riverside Drive. He purchased a yacht, the *Anita Venetian*, a 202-foot steam schooner, and cruised down to Palm Beach to fish and hobnob with the rich at the Breakers Hotel.

Although not directly doing battle, Cutten and Livermore had been on opposite sides of the market. Arthur was desperately selling his wheat and taking a terrible beating, while Jesse was piling up big profits in the mayhem. It was a preview of the titanic wars they would wage over the next two decades.

Seven years younger than Cutten, Livermore became known as the "Boy Plunger" because of his massive and lightning-fast trades in the market. At fourteen, he had run away from home to escape working on his father's farm. He got a job at Paine Webber in Boston as a board boy, posting stock prices on a chalkboard, and then started trading in bucket shops where he proved he could outwit the dodgy operators of these establishments.

Jesse Livermore, "Boy Plunger."

Eventually banned from the bucket shops because of his success, Jesse took his winnings to New York to trade on the legitimate stock exchange. He won and he lost in a series of manoeuvres, learning the sometimes painful lessons that would guide him in his roller-coaster career. In five years, he had a $100,000 stake, which he used to mount his campaign during the panic of 1907.

Cutten and Livermore were two very different characters, sharing only a wary regard for each other's trading abilities. Cutten was understated, methodical, and controlled; he worked long hours and maintained a straight-laced lifestyle; and he patiently built up his wealth over many years. Livermore, in contrast, was flamboyant, impetuous, and mercurial; he enjoyed his nightclubs, showgirls, and yachts; and he lived a boom-and-bust life, making sudden fortunes and just as quickly losing everything.

Livermore was dashing, with movie-star good looks, and was a notorious womanizer. His blond hair was combed back. He wore double-breasted suits from Savile Row. He rode in a canary yellow Rolls-Royce and had his own Pullman car. He was a hard drinker and chain-smoked Cuban cigars.

J.L. would often trade on premonitions. In 1906, for example, he shorted Union Pacific (selling shares borrowed from his broker, betting that he would be able to buy them back later at lower prices, thus making a profit). He couldn't explain why. It was just a feeling he had. And then an earthquake devastated San Francisco. The tall towers in the financial district collapsed. Homes were swallowed. Fires from ruptured gas mains burned across the city. When it was over, hundreds of people had lost their lives. More than half of the 410,000 residents were left homeless, and twenty-five thousand buildings were reduced to rubble. Within days, shares of Union Pacific tumbled. Livermore covered his short position and walked away with a cool $250,000 in profit.[3]

While Livermore would be Cutten's greatest adversary, James A. Patten was the man he most respected and admired. For Arthur, Patten was a sort of father figure, someone he modelled himself after, a heroic alternative to his own weak and disgraced father.

Jim Patten was one of the biggest speculators in the Chicago pits during the first decade of the twentieth century. "He was credited with being the only man ever to corner all four markets of wheat, oats, corn and cotton," the *Chicago Tribune* wrote of him.[4] Arthur studied him carefully, learning from his moves and emulating his trading methods. And Patten, intrigued with this earnest fellow, took him under his wing and became his mentor and friend.

James Patten, commodities speculator and mentor to Cutten.

"I have never known a better man," said Cutten. "He was honorable in every fiber. He never did a mean or a tricky thing in his life. In his biggest deals he had time to be thoughtful of the little fellows who followed his trading operations with piker bets of their own."[5]

In one of their skirmishes in the grain pits, Cutten recalled with some humour how he had won a rare victory over Patten. Contrary to the prevailing wisdom at the Chicago Board of Trade, Cutten was accumulating corn futures during the early summer of 1912. Almost everyone else was a seller. "It seemed to me I was betting against the world that time," he recalled. But the hot dry weather in Kansas convinced him that prices would move up.

In the trading pit, a broker was offering corn. "Sell 100," he shouted (meaning 100,000 bushels) and then through hand gestures indicated a price.

"Take it," Cutten answered and bid for more. He placed his palms in front of his face, signalling that he was a buyer.

Jim Patten's broker jumped in, palms outward, and sold him another six hundred contracts.

"You tell Patten I'll take all he'll sell me," Cutten challenged.

In an office across the street, Patten was on the line with his broker. "Who's been buying my corn?" Hearing that Cutten was the purchaser, he decided to teach the fool a lesson. "Sell him another three hundred."

In a few minutes that Saturday morning, Cutten acquired contracts for a million bushels of corn at 64⅞ cents a bushel. In the pits, they were laughing at him. He was going up against Patten, and Patten was the king.

At the end of trading, Arthur crossed LaSalle Street and entered the offices of Bartlett, Frazier & Co. Patten was there seated before the quotation board. Herbert Ryecroft, president of the firm, was decidedly bearish, and was saying so when Cutten walked in.

"You're dead wrong about corn," said Cutten.

"You'll see it sell at fifty-five," Ryecroft chided.

"It'll sell at eighty," Cutten maintained.

Patten scowled across the top of his glasses. A few days later, he had to buy back the corn from Cutten at 68⅞ cents, a loss of four cents a bushel, or $40,000. Good thing he did. The price continued to rise, and in August cash corn sold for eighty-three cents.[6]

Jim Patten: Running the Corners

THE MAN WHO RAISED THE PRICE OF BREAD

James M. Patten, of Chicago, whose operations in wheat caused a marked increase in the price of flour, and for a time caused talk of the advisability of removing the duty on Canadian wheat as a means of breaking the "corner." The significance of Mr. Patten's operations is discussed on page 30 of this issue

Patten, "The Man Who Raised
the Price of Bread."

Jim Patten was born near Sandwich, Illinois, in 1852, where his parents ran a general store. When his father died of tuberculosis in 1863, Jim went to live with his maternal grandfather, George Beveridge, an ardent abolitionist whose farm served as a station on the "Underground Railroad" used by African Americans escaping slavery.

In 1874, his uncle John Beveridge, then governor of Illinois, got him a job as a clerk with the state grain inspection department in Chicago. He then worked in Montreal selling grain for G.P. Comstock & Company and, following the firm's failure, returned to Chicago to set up his own business with his brother George. By the early 1880s, the Pattens were buying and shipping grain to New England.

On 9 April 1885, he married Amanda Buchanan. They had four children (one died in infancy), and the family moved to Evanston where Jim built a large house – twenty-two rooms, eight bathrooms, fifteen fireplaces, a grand ballroom, and a stable that became a ten-car garage.

In 1901, Jim was elected mayor of Evanston and served one term. Over the next ten years, he and his brother George undertook a series of extraordinary campaigns in the futures markets. They maintained an extensive network of correspondents across the country who provided them with regular reports on growing conditions and weather patterns, and Jim would often travel hundreds of miles to inspect crops in the field. "The real raw material of the speculator is information," Jim remarked.[7]

Their first major foray was in oats, cornering the market and driving the price from thirty-four cents to sixty-five cents a bushel in 1902. This was followed by a $2 million coup in corn.

Then, in 1908, the brothers started to buy up wheat at about ninety cents a bushel, eventually gaining control of more than 20 million bushels. Heavy frosts damaged the crops in both Argentina and Canada, and worldwide shortages ensued. By May 1909, wheat was trading at $1.34. The Pattens made millions, but they were also blamed for the rising cost of bread. Prices rose from five to ten cents a loaf, and there were fears of riots in the cities.[8]

US attorney general George Wickersham launched an investigation into their dealings, and Representative Charles

Scott from Kansas introduced a bill to prohibit futures trading in food products. Jim's house in Evanston was targeted by a bomb scare, and he had to hire bodyguards. He was vilified in sermons and brutally caricatured in newspaper cartoons.[9] He was even the subject of a film by D.W. Griffith titled *A Corner in Wheat*, in which a greedy speculator is justly punished for his sins against society by being buried alive under tons of grain.

Undeterred by the criticism, the Pattens went on to orchestrate another corner, this time in cotton. When Jim visited the Manchester Cotton Exchange in England in March 1910, he was confronted by floor traders who hissed and booed and chased him from the building. Angry that some English mills had been forced to close because of high prices, and fearing that Patten had come to play his games on their turf, they ran after him in the street, and only with the help of police was he able to escape in a carriage. "Although unhurt, Patten was greatly surprised and irritated at the dislike shown by the people of Manchester," it was reported in a dispatch from London.[10]

George died later that year. Jim continued to trade on the CBOT but never again on such a colossal scale. He turned his attention to his various philanthropic interests. He gave more than $1 million to Northwestern University for various projects, including the construction of the original Patten Gymnasium. He donated to hospitals and old-age homes.

By 1925, Arthur Cutten had established himself as the dominant force in Chicago and was starting to build a reputation as the leading bull in New York. Patten was proud of his protégé and marvelled at his knack for picking winners. He noted that Cutten "has been long on stocks that went to sensational highs," and he ascribed this success, at least in part, to Cutten's "extraordinary ability to get inside information."[11]

Arthur would try to get Jim to participate in his market operations. "Get yourself some Montgomery Ward," he urged.

"No, sir," Patten replied. "I'm past speculating."

Cutten would then tease the old gentleman. "Well, I guess that's a good thing. Speculating means worry. You save yourself a lot of trouble."

"Trouble? Do you call it trouble when 70,000 shares of your stock go up 10 points in a day?"

They laughed, but the point was made. It was now Cutten's time.

"Twenty years ago, I was afraid of nothing, but today, if I had a deal like that of my friend, I might not sleep well at night," Patten remarked.[12]

On 24 November 1928, Jim attended the Army-Nebraska football game at Michie Stadium, an outdoor stadium on the campus of the US Military Academy in West Point, New York. Sitting in the cold autumn air, he caught a chill. Two weeks later he died of pneumonia.

His death occurred a day after the old Board of Trade building, slated for demolition, closed its doors. He had spent much of his life within its walls. "It seems like they were fated to go together – the old building and old Jim," a veteran trader observed.[13]

He was buried in the family vault at Oak Mound Cemetery in Sandwich. For James Patten, life itself was a huge bet. "We all are gamblers in this narrow margin of the universe we call the earth," he once observed.[14]

CHAPTER FOUR

Sunny Acres, Movers and Shakers

Although Cutten had been born and raised in the town of Guelph and knew little of farming, he had for many years wished to live in the country. And so, in 1911, he began to assemble several parcels of land and plan a rural retreat outside of Chicago. Located twenty-five miles west of the city, near the village of Downers Grove, the eight-hundred-acre property became an agricultural showpiece with the money he lavished on it.

Marked by two stone pillars, the entrance to the farm was on the south side of Butterfield Road, east of what is today Route 53. Coming through the gates, one first encountered the caretaker's house, a water tower and windmill immediately to the left. Then a little distance to the right, a red brick driveway led to the residence.

Cutten retained Frank Lloyd Wright to design the house. Wright produced a number of drawings (referenced as project #1115 by the Frank Lloyd Wright Foundation) but for some reason did not build the project.[1] It was Ephram Norman Brydges, a Chicago architect, who eventually oversaw the planning and construction of the fifteen-room mansion and the adjoining three-car garage with chauffeur's quarters above.[2]

The house sat on a hill, known locally as Strong's Hill after the original settler Eliphalet Strong,[3] and was built of granite from the area. The floor plan was cross-shaped with intersecting wings. Rooms were panelled or trimmed in oak. The living room featured ceiling beams and a massive fireplace, and from the French doors one could see the formal garden with its pergola and urns. There was also a greenhouse and orchard nearby.

A tree-lined lane ran down the hill to the south, jogged west to run parallel with a creek, then south again over a bridge to the farm

Sunny Acres, Cutten's residence.

buildings. These consisted of the farm manager's house and garage, a boarding house for the hired hands, a three-storey hay barn flanked by two silos, barns for the various livestock, an office, machine shed, and second water tower and windmill. All the buildings were painted white and trimmed in green and had wood shingle roofs.

Cutten insisted that it was not an estate but a working farm. Naming it Sunny Acres, he grew corn, oats, and wheat in the fields. There were 80 head of cattle, 20 horses, 500 hogs, as well as sheep, ducks, and chickens.[4] The farm produced milk, wool, eggs, meat, fruits, vegetables, and a small amount of wine. What was not consumed on the property was sold to Pitcher's Market in Downers Grove, while the surplus milk went to the creamery in Lisle.

Half a dozen people worked year-round on the farm, with extra help hired during the crop seasons. James Nelson was the manager, and he was paid sixty-five dollars a month and provided with a house.[5] Other full-time staff included a caretaker/gardener, a dairyman, manager of

Dining room (top) and living room (bottom), main residence, Sunny Acres.

Hay barn and twin silos, Sunny Acres.

the horse barn, and a couple of farm hands. This was in addition to the butler, cook, maid, and driver who kept things running smoothly at the residence.

Arthur loved the farm and spent as much time there as he could. It gave him "a strange and deep comfort ... something that must have been important to my ancestors, for it throbs in my blood."[6] The Cuttens lived at Sunny Acres, and most business days he commuted into the city either in his chauffeured limousine or on the Chicago Aurora and Elgin train.

Out in the country, he dressed in knickers and knee socks and wore a tweed cap. On summer weekends he would bring guests out from the city, and they would go horseback riding. In addition to the farmlands, there were great wooded areas that had been planted with oak, spruce, poplar, and birch, and majestic views of the East Branch of the DuPage River, which flowed through the property.

He enjoyed the company of the men who worked for him. He would come down to see his manager James Nelson, and they would talk on a first-name basis and laugh together. Arthur would occasionally give him shares of stock and tell him, "Play around with it, see what you can do, but don't tell Maud!" Or he would be there when Harry Sutter, the blacksmith, came to do the horseshoeing.

Cutten and "Chick" Evans on their way to California in 1917.

His neighbour to the south was Joy Morton, founder of the Morton Salt Company. The Morton estate, named Thornhill, had been built a few years earlier. To the east was fuel oil and coal magnate John Berryman. To the west was Walter Rogers, president of engineering and contracting firm Bates and Rogers Construction Company, whose family would often join the Cuttens on Friday nights for dinner.[7]

The Chicago Golf Club was only a few miles away in Wheaton, and Arthur joined this very exclusive club. Along with making money in the markets and farming, golfing was one of his few true passions. He also played at the Edgewater Golf Club on Chicago's North Side, where he met and befriended Charles "Chick" Evans in 1913. Evans was one of the top golfers in the country and would go on to win both the US Amateur and US Open three years later. Chick must have helped Arthur with his game, for Cutten would later recall: "He made me a better golfer than a man [of my age] has any right to be."[8]

Without any offspring of their own, the Cuttens found other ways to fill their lives. Maud threw herself into child welfare causes. Arthur funded various youth charities, including a program that Chick Evans established to provide college scholarships to golf caddies.

When Maud's sister Permelia died in 1915 at the age of thirty-four, she left a husband, George Shirley, and two young children, Ruth and Joseph.[9] The Cuttens had always doted on the youngsters, and now they stepped in to aid and support them.[10] Arthur was especially proud of the lad who seemed keen on following in his famous uncle's footsteps. After Joseph graduated from the University of Illinois, Cutten arranged a position for him at a prestigious brokerage firm in Toronto.[11]

They also treated Arthur's younger brother Harry, a life-long bachelor who would stay with them at Sunny Acres for extended periods, with special affection. Arthur's two sisters, Lenore and Constance, remained in Guelph, and his two other brothers, Lionel and Ralph (Edward had died in 1912), had families and careers in Toronto. Lionel was part owner of a company that sold car accessories and radios and manufactured drapes. Ralph was a partner in the mortgage brokerage firm Cutten and Chudleigh. They were very close, all of them, frequently visiting each other.

In July 1915, their father died at Tranquille. Walter Hoyt had never recovered after the failure of his bank and had lived the remainder of his years in quiet eclipse. He was laid to rest in the family plot at Woodlawn Cemetery in Guelph. Six years later, their mother Annie Margaretta was buried beside him.

Always eager to please the citizens of Guelph, Arthur sprinkled his money about his hometown. He contributed to the building of the new YMCA and later paid off its mortgage of $20,000. After his father's death, he gave $10,000 to the cemetery for various improvements, including a new wrought iron fence, entrance gates, and other enhancements.[12]

On 14 July 1916, Arthur became a naturalized citizen of the United States. He was forty-six and had lived twenty-six of those years in his adopted land. When asked by a reporter whether he identified more as a Canadian or an American, he replied: "Neither ... We come from the same stock and we think the same kind of thoughts. [We] are very much the same people."[13]

With war in Europe, wheat and other grains began a steady upward climb. Cutten was already a millionaire, and now he would increase his wealth many times over. *Time* magazine reported that he was "said to have made more money than any other individual operator" during this period. In 1916, for example, he bought wheat for about one dollar a bushel. By September, prices were fifty cents higher, and he made $1.2 million on that single deal.

By the time the US joined the Allies in 1917, prices had soared. Cash wheat was at $3.47, corn at $2.36, and oats at 85 cents. In support of the war effort, the federal government asked the Chicago Board of Trade and other grain exchanges to stop trading wheat futures beginning 1 September 1917. The halt lasted almost three years.

At the war's end, the US economy went into a slump. European demand for US goods and foodstuffs declined, leaving factories and farmers with large surpluses. And of course, when the exchanges resumed trading in wheat, prices plummeted. This sparked anger on the farms, and Midwest legislators blamed the speculators on LaSalle

Street for the collapse. Senator Arthur Capper of Kansas, an outspoken critic of the Board of Trade, charged that it ran "the most wanton and most destructive game of chance in the world."[14]

Although he preferred life at Sunny Acres and the company of his closest friends and family members, Cutten knew many of Chicago's most prominent citizens and occasionally moved in their circles. Southern California was a favoured destination for the wealthy, and the Cuttens spent winters there in the company of such men (and their wives) as: Colonel John Lambert, one of the largest shareholders in US Steel; George Marcy, president of Armour Grain Company; Robert Carr, president of Dearborn Chemical Company; and grain trader James Rankin.

In January 1917, Arthur and Maud travelled on the Santa Fe Railway's "de-Luxe" to Pasadena.[15] They had a private drawing room, slept in a brass bed, and took their meals in a well-appointed dining car. On arrival, they checked into the Hotel Maryland. Most days Arthur played golf, usually at the Midwick Country Club, where he was a member,[16] and evenings were reserved for dinner parties.

Another year, again in Pasadena, the Cuttens hosted a dinner dance at the Hotel Huntington for 125 guests. The menu included imported English pheasants rushed by express from New York, and the ballroom was adorned with thousands of American Beauty roses. The elaborate affair cost an estimated eight thousand dollars.[17]

When Colonel Lambert died in 1922, his funeral was attended by top bankers, company presidents, steel barons, and political leaders from across the country. Three former governors were there, as was Robert Todd Lincoln (President Abraham Lincoln's son). Arthur Cutten was one of the honorary pallbearers.[18]

In Chicago, the Cuttens kept a pied-à-terre at 209 Lake Shore Drive on the Gold Coast. They used it to entertain when in the city or as a place for Arthur to stay when working late downtown. One of his key commodities brokers, Allan M. Clement, kept an apartment in the same building and had an office located across from Cutten's hideout on LaSalle Street. His wife Grace was a friend of Maud's, and the two women were active in raising money for the Home for Destitute Crippled Children.

Arthur S. Jackson, head of commission house Jackson Bros. & Co. (later Jackson Bros., Boesel & Co.), also managed various accounts for Arthur. He and his wife Louise were close to the Cuttens, and they vacationed together in Florida.[19]

Arthur loved horses, and occasionally he and Maud would attend the big races at Arlington Park, where he was a member of the Post and Paddock Club. His old chum Tom Wilson was a director of the club, and they would have lunch together and bet on the "ponies."

Edson White, who had boarded with Arthur when they were young men, had gone on to become president of Armour & Company. He and his wife Lillian attended the theatre and opera with the Cuttens.

Cutten also hobnobbed with John J. Mitchell, president of the Illinois Trust and Savings Bank (later the Illinois Merchants Trust Co.) and George M. Reynolds, chairman of Continental Illinois Bank and Trust. Both bankers were part of the Pasadena crowd, and Mitchell also played the links at the Midwick Club.[20]

Others friends and business associates included: Bernard A. Eckhart, multi-millionaire businessman; Harrison Riley, president of Chicago Title and Trust Company; Alfred Martin, vice-president of Bartlett Frazier & Co.; and Harry H. Lobdell, partner in brokerage firm Lamson Brothers & Company.

CHAPTER FIVE

Robbery and Retribution

In 1920, prohibition came into force. The Volstead Act made the production, sale, and transport of "intoxicating liquors" illegal. But rather than ushering in a new era of morality, the 18th Amendment resulted in increased crime and lawlessness as gangs fought to control the lucrative trade. Bootlegging became a big business, and gangsters got rich. Murder, bribery, and corruption were rampant.

In Chicago, Al Capone was the boss. Law enforcement officials and politicians were on his payroll. The competition was brutally eliminated. And, under his protection, smugglers moved huge quantities of alcohol across the border, using fast cars and boats to deliver their cargo. The production of liquor was legal in Canada, and Chicago became a major hub for the import and distribution of Canadian whisky.

Prohibition also helped shape the culture of the 1920s. With much of the public flouting the law, it became acceptable – even glamourous – to challenge the conventional. Flappers appeared, the Charleston was the rage, hip flasks and raccoon coats were in, and jazz bands wailed and whooped in the underground clubs.

At his farm near Downers Grove, Arthur Cutten was in bed by 10:00 p.m. and up every morning at 6:30 a.m. He was old school, conservative, and temperate.

And while he rarely imbibed, he kept cases of liquor in a vault in his cellar. It was for entertaining guests, he said, purchased before prohibition. "If I lived a century, I would not drink so much."[1] But his stash of scotch, gin, bourbon, and champagne – worth thousands – was a temptation for others. Especially when premium hootch commanded top dollar in the speakeasies.

Late afternoon, Monday, 27 March 1922. Five men sat in the automobile, a Haynes Model 55 Touring Car, parked well back but with a good view of arriving passengers.[2] They waited. Finally, the train came into the Glen Ellyn station, and they watched as Arthur Cutten stepped to the platform. Right on time.

They watched as Cutten, in a dark dress coat and carrying a newspaper, walked to his limousine. The chauffeur had the door open. He climbed in, and they sped off.

"Here we go," said Simon Rosenberg as he eased the Haynes out onto the road and followed. It had been raining earlier, and the road was slick with mud.

Cutten's chauffeur, Morton Hollis, had driven this route hundreds of times and knew every twist and turn. He roared ahead.

"We're losing him," said Hart O'Malley, the front-seat passenger. He held a revolver in his hand. In the back, Otto Tempera, Peter Cuda, and Joseph Vormittag, also armed with handguns, were silent.

They had planned to kidnap Cutten by overtaking his limo and forcing it off the road. But Rosenberg was having trouble keeping up. The sun was setting. He pushed harder on the accelerator, and the Haynes went into a skid and slid into the ditch.

At Sunny Acres, Cutten came through the front door and shouted a pleasant greeting. It had been a fine day. He held a long line of wheat, and prices were moving up. He joined Maud and his brother Harry in the living room where they sat near the glowing fireplace. It was good to be home.

On Butterfield Road an obliging farmer had pulled the Haynes out of the ditch with his tractor. The gang of five considered their options and decided to proceed to the Cutten farm. Their game now was robbery. They would hold up the inhabitants, ransack the house, and fence the stolen property through their accomplices in Chicago. Easy money and less risky than kidnapping.

They also had an "inside" man. Joe Vormittag, the youngest member of the criminal group, had worked as a houseboy in the Cutten residence. He knew the layout of the estate, the schedules of the servants, the habits of the family. And he knew about the valuable liquor in the cellar. Vormittag had quit his job about a year earlier and had gone about shopping this information to various underworld characters. Participants were recruited, Rosenberg became the leader, and the enterprise went forward.

At about 6:30 p.m., the bandits pulled into the driveway of the Cutten farm, circled the residence, and halted at the rear. John Johnson, the butler, was in the yard.

"Can you give us a little gas?" asked Rosenberg from the car.

Johnson approached. "Sure thing. We've got a spare tank in the garage. I'll get it."

Before he could turn, a revolver was shoved in his face. "Don't make a sound or I'll blow your head off. Now take us to the house."

Pushing Johnson in front of them, the gang members walked up to the back door. Through a window, they could see the Cuttens having dinner together.

They rushed inside, through the kitchen, and into the dining room, waving their guns and shouting. "Stay where you are! Don't move!" They rounded up the household staff – Naomi Larson the maid, Marie Larson the cook, along with Johnson the butler – and made them stand with the three Cuttens against the wall.

Outside, Max Bergholt the gardener and Hollis the chauffeur drove up in a Ford truck used on the farm. They had come at the appointed time for their evening meal and were unaware of the situation unfolding in the house. They were quickly corralled and brought in to stand with the rest.

The bandits methodically stripped their victims of every bit of cash and jewellery. When a twenty-five-dollar watch was taken from the maid, Arthur protested. "Aw, you can buy her another one," a gang member sneered.

Their eyes lit up when they saw the splendid jewellery Maud was wearing. "Off with it, bitch." They roughly pulled the sapphire and diamond rings from her fingers, tore the platinum watch from her wrist, and plucked the string of pearls from her neck. For Arthur, the only tolerable moment in the entire ordeal was knowing that the pearl necklace was an imitation.

None of the thieves wore a mask. But because Vormittag might be recognized, he tried to conceal himself by keeping his head averted, coat collar pulled up, and hat pulled down as he moved about the house.

A gun at his spine, Arthur was marched upstairs where he was made to lie face down on his bed while Rosenberg and O'Malley searched closets, drawers, and chests. They found US Treasury notes and silver and gold coins, along with a Remington rifle and two handguns. They used Arthur's golf bag to carry the loot.

Then, assembling their prisoners, the gangsters herded everyone into the basement where they knew the liquor was stored. Arthur was ordered to open the vault. "Be quick about it or I'll start shooting people," Rosenberg threatened.

Arthur fumbled nervously and unsuccessfully.

Losing patience, Rosenberg stepped in, twirling the combination lock as Cutten read off the numbers that he had written high up on one of the supporting columns. The door swung open. Cases of liquor were stacked inside. The robbers moved the crates upstairs and loaded them into the Ford truck. Ripping open other boxes, they cursed when they discovered fruit preserves.

"Alright, everyone in," Rosenberg gestured with his gun, motioning the prisoners into the vault.

"We'll smother in there," Arthur objected. The vault was air tight, reinforced with thick cement walls and protected by a steel door.

"We'll telephone after we get away and have someone come and let you out."

"But all in the household are here," Arthur insisted. "Besides, we'll be dead before anyone can get those doors open. Eight people in that small space ..."

"Get moving, you!"

As the door clanged shut, Arthur was certain that they had been locked up to die. There would be no telephone call. The inhabitants of Sunny Acres had been buried alive.

The gang transferred the stolen goods to the faster Haynes, and Rosenberg, O'Malley, and Cuda took off in the car. Vormittag and Tempera fled in the boosted Ford truck. They headed east towards the city.

In the vault, Johnson withdrew a small steel ruler from his vest pocket. It had been a gift from Cutten, and he carried it everywhere. Using it now as a screwdriver, he worked quickly to remove four screws from a metal plate on the door. This exposed the locking mechanism and, one by one, he was able to release the bolts. They pushed hard against the door and it opened.

DuPage County sheriff George Leineke pointing to the buckshot holes in the back of the farm truck used by the robbers at Sunny Acres, 1922.

Johnson and Hollis rushed to the garage. The chauffeur fired up the Dodge roadster, and the butler jumped in, armed with a double-barrelled shotgun. They raced up the lane, took a fast right onto Butterfield Road, and tore off in pursuit.

Six miles and ten minutes later, they caught up with the Ford. Johnson opened fire, riddling it with buckshot. The truck screeched to a halt. The two gangsters leaped out and ran into a cornfield. When Johnson and Hollis pulled up, all they found were drops of blood and a man's hat on the roadside near the abandoned vehicle.

Meanwhile, Arthur had telephoned the police and had also called his neighbour Joy Morton to warn him of the danger. The police set up roadblocks and stopped and questioned all motorists heading into Chicago that night, but the gang members eluded the authorities and remained at large.

The three Cuttens, badly shaken, gathered in the living room. Discussing the harrowing events of the evening, Maud mentioned that one of the robbers – the one who tried to conceal himself – seemed familiar. He appeared to know his way around the house, where the light switches were located, where the passageways led. And then it struck her. She felt certain it was a former houseboy, Joe. This information was passed on to the police.

Lieutenant Axel Jensen of the Chicago police department was assigned the case. He was able to trace the hat found near the stolen truck to a shop on Fullerton Avenue and, from there, confirm that it had been sold to one Joseph Vormittag. Maud's suspicions were correct.

Within a week, Vormittag was in custody. He was nursing a shotgun wound and immediately confessed. In addition to those who carried out the robbery, he named five others who he said were involved in helping to plan and assist in the crime – Casper Rosenberg (Simon's brother), Paul Grabowski, John Glowinski, Gustav Kawell, and Joseph Cornelison.

Otto Tempera, also wounded by the butler's shotgun blast, was arrested next. Then, in quick succession, Grabowski, Glowinski, Kawell, and Cornelison were scooped up (charges against the latter two were dismissed).

Vormittag served two years at the state reformatory in Pontiac. Tempera was sent to the state penitentiary at Joliet and was paroled after three years. Grabowski and Glowinski received minor jail terms.

Police and some of the gang members involved in the robbery at Sunny Acres.
Left to right: Lieutenant Axel Jensen, Gustav Kawell, Sergeant
William Schultz, Joseph Cornelison, Paul Grabowski, Sergeant John Hardy,
Otto Tempera, Joseph Vormittag.

But the remaining four – Simon and Casper Rosenberg, Hart O'Malley, and Peter Cuda – had escaped the dragnet and were in the wind.

The stolen property was valued at about $40,000, and none of it was ever recovered. After the robbery, the Cutten home was put under strong guard. Arthur also took to keeping a pistol tucked under the cushion of his favourite chair "should the need ever arise."

He announced a $1,000 reward for information leading to the arrest of the remaining fugitives, and he vowed to pursue them until all were captured and brought to justice. "I will catch those men if it takes the rest of my life, and I will use every dollar at my command," he told reporters. "The loss of the property is not so important, but they used profanity in the presence of my wife and locked us in a vault where we might have suffocated. That was an unnecessary, fiendish piece of cruelty. It filled me with rage."

Cutten financed the manhunt himself, hiring an army of private detectives to run down every lead and follow every trail.

By the end of the year, O'Malley and Cuda had been caught, each receiving a sentence of ten years to life at Joliet. "It was a satisfaction to me each time I knew that prison doors had closed behind another of these men," Cutten commented.

Alfred "Jake" Lingle, veteran police reporter for the *Chicago Tribune*, knew all the important mobsters, politicians, prosecutors, judges, and cops in the city. He had interviewed Al Capone several times and wore a diamond-studded belt buckle said to be a gift from Capone. He was close to Police Commissioner William Russell and Assistant Attorney General Harry Ash. He hobnobbed with Governor Emmerson. And he counted Arthur Cutten among his friends.

Cutten had met Lingle and Commissioner Russell at a golf course in Biloxi, Mississippi, one winter and had played a round with them. Cutten recalled that the newspaper man was a terrible golfer, stepping up to the ball and in one motion trying to hit it like he was playing baseball. Lingle became a frequent guest at Sunny Acres, and he would often drop by Cutten's office on LaSalle Street. The millionaire trader would talk about his ongoing manhunt, and the reporter would speak casually about the underworld he was covering.

"You had better be careful of those people," said Cutten.

"Aw, that's my job. I can't get information for my newspaper about crime unless I know the big criminals, and crime has become a major industry in Chicago. Don't sell crime short," Lingle joked.[3]

Because of his connections, Lingle became a key figure in helping Cutten track down the Rosenberg brothers. He squeezed his contacts, passed on any relevant information he dug up, and assisted in selecting the detectives to work on the case.[4] In return, he received stock tips from Cutten. His heaviest investments included Simmons

Chicago Tribune *reporter Jake Lingle. He helped Cutten run down
the gang members who robbed Sunny Acres.*

*Simon Rosenberg, leader of the gang
that robbed Arthur Cutten.*

Company and Sinclair Oil, two stocks closely associated with the famous speculator.

It took eight years for the Rosenbergs to be nabbed. Simon was arrested on 6 April 1930. Cutten's detectives followed him from the Pacific Coast to the Atlantic, from the Gulf of Mexico to Canada, finally nabbing him in Cleveland. "I've led a dog's life in fear of arrest every minute," Simon told the court. He pleaded guilty and was sent to Joliet.

Also tired of running, Casper surrendered three months later. He walked into the office of the State's Attorney of DuPage County and announced: "I'm Casper Rosenberg, and I think you're looking for me. For eight years I've been in hell. I can't go on hiding forever. Cutten wins."

On hearing that the last fugitive was in custody, Cutten exulted: "Well, that's over." He had kept his promise and exacted his revenge.

In court at the sentencing of Simon Rosenberg. Left to right: Margaret Morton,
Maud Cutten, Arthur Cutten, and Joy Morton.

"I never give up. When a man comes into my house and robs me and
my family and locks us in a vault where we might suffocate, I keep on
until I get him."[5]

And then when it was done, he showed compassion. He asked the
state prosecutor to drop charges against Casper, who he felt had re-
formed and become a law-abiding citizen. Casper had been living with
his family in a small town in Michigan where he was a successful real
estate agent.

"Send him back where he is building a character for himself," Cutten
urged. The charges were dismissed and Casper was freed.

Simon, too, was treated kindly. At his parole hearing in 1931, Cutten
supported his release. Simon had married in 1926, had two daughters,
and worked as an insurance salesman in Cleveland. Parole was granted.

CHAPTER SIX

Wheat King

With the economy beginning to improve following the recession of 1920–21, Cutten embarked upon his most daring operation to date. He no longer did his own trading at the exchange. He was now speculating on such a large scale that, to be successful, he had to conduct his business in absolute secrecy. He explained that he had "little faith in the ability or disposition of other people to keep their mouths shut."[1] And so he traded through half a dozen different brokerage houses and many different accounts, making it difficult for anyone to get a clear picture of his activities or overall position.

By April 1922, he had accumulated futures contracts for some 6 to 8 million bushels of wheat. It seemed he had cornered the market as prices advanced to $1.45. His plan was to take delivery, reasoning that the sellers would be unable to deliver such quantities under the contract terms and would be forced to settle with him at higher prices.

The main sellers were two large elevator operators – J. Rosenbaum Grain Company, headed up by Emanuel F. Rosenbaum, and Armour Grain Company, owned by J. Ogden Armour, who had taken over the company upon the death of his father P.D. Armour.

Trying to extricate themselves from Cutten's grip, executives of these two firms met with the directors of the Board of Trade and persuaded them that Chicago's grain elevators were full and that, therefore, it was necessary to invoke the emergency delivery rule. This allowed the sellers to fulfill their contracts more quickly and easily by delivering the wheat in railway cars within fifty miles of Chicago rather than at elevators as ordinarily required.

On 9 May, a day after the emergency rule was declared, wheat sank to $1.32 on reports that large trainloads of wheat were bound for the city. Holders of May futures began liquidating, and prices dropped to

Jonathan Ogden Armour, president of Armour & Company.

$1.16 a bushel. Those who took delivery were having to pay demurrage of five dollars a day per freight car (a penalty charged for the use of cars that have not been unloaded after a reasonable period), and, faced with these costs, they were forced to sell at tremendous losses.

Close to eight thousand rail cars of wheat stood on track around Chicago, much of it Cutten's. Although he "lost plenty," he was able to avoid a complete catastrophe by loading his wheat onto boats and shipping it eastward to elevators in Buffalo and other ports. "Although I could hold on to my wheat by shipping it out of Chicago, many others were less fortunate."[2] Cutten maintained that Armour and Rosenbaum had fabricated the story about the lack of storage space and had enlisted the support and cooperation of the Board of Trade in protecting their interests.

Testifying before the Federal Trade Commission on 12 October 1922, he downplayed his market clout by claiming he was just "a cash grain merchant and dirt farmer" and claimed he would have made a profit had it not been for the large elevator firms conspiring against him.

The truth was, he had been outwitted and outplayed. It was a lesson he would not forget.

The sharp break in wheat prices in 1922 provided a powerful incentive for Congress to pass the Grain Futures Act. Legislators had tried a year earlier to regulate the market with the Future Trading Act, but the Supreme Court had ruled its use of a tax to enforce compliance was unconstitutional. The Grain Futures Act instead relied on Congress's jurisdiction over interstate commerce, and it was upheld by the court.

Seventy-five years after the Chicago Board of Trade was established, the act ushered in the first federal regulation of grain futures trading in the US. It put in place a number of measures aimed at eliminating speculative excesses and price manipulation, including the power to designate contract markets, the creation of an administrative agency to investigate abuses, and disclosure of trading information.

Board of Trade members hated this meddling in what they considered their private affairs. They claimed it would cause irreparable harm to the exchange and to them personally, drive large bullish speculators from the market, destroy legitimate hedging, and depress grain prices for farmers.

What irked them most were the new reporting rules. The legislation required anyone buying or selling futures contracts totalling 500,000 bushels or more of wheat, corn, or oats, and 200,000 bushels or more of rye or barley, to report these transactions to the Grain Futures Administration.

No one was more vocal in their opposition to the new law than Arthur Cutten. Because secrecy was vital to successfully building a big position, either long or short, having information about his trading activities in the hands of others represented a significant risk for him.

"The notion that I could buy or sell no more than half a million bushels of grain without having my trades subjected to the scrutiny of government clerks was, to me, galling," he commented.[3]

And while the hoots of protest were loud and the predictions of doom were dire, nothing really changed. The speculators, Cutten among them, largely ignored the legislation. After operating without government oversight for so many years, they assumed – correctly for a time – that there would be little attempt to enforce the law. It was business as usual.

After his failed corner in 1922, Cutten carried out an extraordinary series of campaigns in wheat, corn, and rye that made him one of the richest men in America and ensured that his name was known throughout the country. He bought, owned, and sold more grain than any person who ever operated in the grain pits. His timing couldn't have been better. Worldwide shortages were driving prices upward.

Cutten started in the corn market in 1924. Studying weather maps, he noted that excessive rainfall through the spring had delayed planting. He began buying at forty cents a bushel and took delivery of 4 million bushels in May. By late June the price reached eighty-five cents. He sold his cash corn into consumptive channels and took July contracts in exchange. By mid-July the price hit $1.10 and again he took delivery and sold the physical commodity to customers in the spot market.

Cutten had been right. The cold, wet weather had held back the corn crop. "I began accumulating corn because I believed it would be hard to get. Farmers have not sold their grain owing to the backward spring, receipts have been small all over the country, and consumers have had to come to Chicago to get their supplies," he explained.[4]

By September, he was out of corn. And $1.5 million richer.

Rye, too, was a good bet. He started to buy at seventy-two cents and put together a big line of some 8 million bushels. Late in the year he sold at $1.50.

But his biggest score was in wheat. Beginning in June 1924, he plunged into the market. Buying through many different brokers and dozens of accounts, he gradually put together a long position of about 30 million bushels. His holdings were said to be the largest ever accumulated.

With the US mid-west and Canadian Prairies suffering drought conditions, prices skyrocketed. In October, wheat roared through $1.50.

For the first time, his name began to appear regularly in the press. He was dubbed the "Wheat King" and his fame grew in grain markets around the world. This was not what Cutten wanted as public attention threatened exposure of his operations and greater scrutiny from federal regulators.

But he also found that media celebrity could be used to his advantage. By granting selective interviews and issuing timely statements, he could "bull" the market. And this he did in December 1924 when he publicly forecast that wheat, then selling for May delivery at $1.70, would cross two dollars. His prediction triggered a wave of purchase orders.

It seemed everyone was buying wheat futures. There were press reports of messenger boys, taxi drivers, stenographers, and shopkeepers getting rich. It was the kind of frenzied speculation that would grip the stock market a few years later.

Prices rose to $2.05 in January 1925, the highest level, outside of wartime, in more than fifty years. Cutten's wheat jammed elevators at Chicago and Baltimore, and it was estimated that he was paying $100,000 a month in storage costs and insurance to carry the grain.

In February, Cutten decided he needed a vacation. He and Maud travelled to Miami where he played golf and had his portrait painted by Carol Aus (1868–1934). Norwegian-born, Aus did portraits of many

Painting of Arthur Cutten by Carol Aus, 1925.

of Chicago's elite, and she was popularly known for her *Saturday Evening Post* covers. She was in Miami for an exhibition of her work, and thus the timing was convenient for both sitter and artist.

On Friday, 13 March, there was a sudden break in wheat, with prices slumping to $1.66. The Cuttens were in Baltimore, on their way home,

Jesse Livermore, the Bear of Wall Street and Cutten's long-time adversary.

and Arthur was receiving frantic calls from his brokers. He had to put up $2 million in margin immediately.

The word was that a group of speculators, led by Jesse Livermore, had launched a bear raid. Livermore knew Cutten was travelling, was out of touch with his brokers, and was unable to mount much of a counteroffensive; therefore, it was an opportune time to hammer prices with massive short selling.[5] From his winter retreat at the

Breakers Hotel in Palm Beach, the Boy Plunger coordinated the attack on his old foe.

By the time the Cuttens arrived back in Chicago, the avalanche of selling had driven the price down to $1.64½. On 17 March, it hit $1.51. It was the most sensational drop in the history of the grain trade. Thousands of speculators were wiped out.

Cutten held on, and even increased his holdings, again talking up wheat to the press. Livermore covered his short position as the panic subsided and prices rebounded. Wheat jumped back to two dollars in late March, and Cutten unloaded.

He blamed himself for wrongly betting that wheat would go to $2.50. And he was furious with Livermore and his "clique of professional bears" for timing the assault to take advantage of his absence from the market. But he had escaped a mauling and recouped his profits, making $15 million on his wheat over a nine-month period. The newly crowned Wheat King was at the top of his game. He paid $540,000 in income taxes on his 1924 earnings alone, more than any other individual in the Chicago district, and placing him among the top twenty-five taxpayers in all of the US.[6]

Cutten's growing wealth and fame made him a target. He received "bags of begging letters" pleading for a handout or a market tip. Strangers would "pluck my coat tails or seize my lapels each time I was recognized on the street, in elevators or in corridors. How was I to tell every Tom, Dick and Harry what to buy or what to sell?"[7]

A distant relative made several requests for money, and Arthur complied. Finally, when the solicitations had become an annoying habit, he sent the man a final cheque signed with the advice "now do not let me see you again."[8]

When Chick Evans filed for bankruptcy in federal court in 1923, heading the list of creditors was Arthur Cutten. Chick had been making some disastrous plays in the market and owed his friend and occasional golfing buddy about $200,000. Arthur forgave the debt, with the gentle admonishment to "just keep out of the grain market from now on."

The wild gyrations in the grain markets during 1924–25 caused consternation in the Coolidge administration and prompted calls for further regulation from Congress. Secretary of Agriculture William Jardine ordered an extensive inquiry, and he travelled to Chicago, where he met with CBOT officials. "We are not opposed to the legitimate functioning of the Board of Trade, but we do oppose gambling. People are beginning to think it is a nuisance, because it has been running wild," Jardine told CBOT president Frank Carey and other exchange officials.[9] He pointed out that there was a lot of resentment among farmers, who felt that their crop prices were being manipulated by a small group of speculators who could make more money in one operation than they would earn in a lifetime.

The agriculture secretary made it clear that he expected the board to "clean house" or face new laws and restrictions. He demanded it take action to prevent cornering and bear raids; the dissemination of false, misleading, and inaccurate reports; and erratic and destructive price swings. "A failure on the part of the Board to take these steps immediately will leave me no alternative but to inaugurate action looking to suspension or revocation of the designation of the Chicago Board of Trade as a contract market," Jardine warned.

To avoid more meddling by Washington, the CBOT directors formed the Business Conduct Committee to oversee the trading practices of its members and to curb abuses.

In late 1925, Cutten was back at it. He was long several million bushels of May wheat, which he had purchased at less than $1.50 a bushel, and prices were now at $1.66. There were rumours that he was trying again to corner the market.

The Business Conduct Committee couldn't ignore these developments. It sent a notice to Cutten ordering him to appear before the committee to explain his dealings. The speculator was outraged. "By every right of commerce, I was entitled to a profit on my transactions for the risk I had taken," he fumed.

He crossed LaSalle Street to the Board of Trade building, took the old elevator with its varnished interior and exposed cable to the seventh floor, and entered the chamber. He knew all the committee members. They had been friends and colleagues for years.

"Look, Arthur, the Grain Futures Administration has made a complaint that you are carrying too much open stuff," one of them said.

William M. Jardine, US secretary of agriculture, 1925–29.

Another put his arm across Cutten's shoulders. "You ought to sell some wheat, for the sake of the Board of Trade," he said. "You know, this committee is the device we settled upon to keep the government from taking fuller control of the trading in futures."

Cutten protested vehemently. "I know all that, but is there anything criminal in an honest profit? I'm buying with and risking my own money. Why should I sell before I am ready?"

"For the sake of the Board of Trade," they told him again.

He was disgusted, and said so. But in the end, he threw up his hands and agreed to sell part of his line.

The realization that he was now subject to the whims of others, that kowtowing to politicians and bureaucrats was the new order, filled him with indignation and resentment.

His elevator ride to the seventh floor had been witnessed by the traders in the pits. They quickly concluded that he was being forced to unload part of his position, and they started to sell. By the time Cutten returned to street level, wheat was off four cents and closed down 7¼ cents for the day.

"That elevator ride cost me at least a quarter of a million dollars," he remarked.[10]

Continuing to shower gifts on Guelph, Arthur donated a carillon to St George's Anglican Church. Costing $30,000, the bells were made by Gillett and Johnston at its foundry in Croydon, England. He also paid for a new organ, stained glass windows, carved oak choir stalls, and an electric clock. "Oh, I don't want anything said about that," Cutten told reporters. "I am glad to do this little bit for my old church."[11] When the bells rang at the dedication, Cutten couldn't be there in person, but he listened to the ringing music by phone from Chicago.

In 1926, he commissioned the placement of a huge obelisk in Wood-lawn Cemetery to mark the Cutten family plot. Constructed in Toronto and shipped to Guelph on a railway flatcar, it was thirty-six feet high and weighed more than twenty-five tons. At the time, it was the largest single shaft of granite in Canada.

Arriving at the railway station, the monument was so large that it had to be unloaded onto dollies and then pulled by a team of horses along a temporary rail track into the cemetery.[12] The obelisk, erected in a grove of evergreens, was inscribed with the names of Arthur's father and mother, his brothers Edward and Charles, and his sister Mary. Other names would be added in due time.

Cutten family burial plot and monument, Woodlawn Cemetery, Guelph.

CHAPTER SEVEN

Taking New York

In 1926, Cutten turned his attention to Wall Street. He had dabbled in stocks, almost as a sideline, for years. Now he was going to get very serious about the Big Board. He continued to be an important player in the Chicago pits, but his really spectacular operations would now take place in New York.

There were good reasons for this. The futures market had collapsed because of crop overproduction. The glut had depressed grain prices, and there was little likelihood of any immediate improvement.

As well, Washington was more intent on regulating commodity futures than stocks. Because of the farm vote, there was more political capital for Congress in restricting manipulative trading practices on the grain exchanges than in the securities markets. Cutten saw his activities on the Chicago Board of Trade coming under the increasing scrutiny of bureaucrats from the Grain Futures Administration, while the New York Stock Exchange remained largely unfettered and free of government interference.

On Wall Street, you were not required to submit records to a government agency, there were no limits on the number of shares you could trade, and there were no rules prohibiting corners. It was still largely a wide open, no-holds-barred game. That's where the action was, so that's where Cutten would play.

"I like to make money," he acknowledged. "There is a thrill in the actual process unequalled by any emotion a man of my years is apt to experience. I shan't deny that fascination; I shan't assert any hypocritical folderol about the good one can do with money. I have made it because I like to make it."[1] By this time, the Wheat King had taken an estimated $30 million to $50 million out of the grain markets. As Bull

Cutten of Wall Street, his wealth would be vastly augmented over the next three years.

His first big score was in Baldwin Locomotive Works, the largest locomotive manufacturer in the US. Cutten targeted the company because there was an exceptionally small float (small number of shares available on the market) and heavy short selling. He reasoned that a technical corner could be created by buying up the stock, reducing the floating supply, and panicking the bears into covering their positions at ever higher prices.

At the same time, the seven Fisher brothers of Detroit were interested in Baldwin. They had sold their Fisher Body Corporation to General Motors for some $235 million in cash and GM stock, and they wanted to put their money to work in the market. Along with Cutten, they began quietly accumulating Baldwin shares. The two camps operated separately but in a coordinated fashion.

Their initial purchases were at around one hundred dollars a share, rising to $115 through the summer of 1926. The buying was carried out through various accounts, several brokerage offices, and in small share lots so as not to arouse suspicion. Then, in November, Baldwin soared upward as the shorts scrambled to cover (buy back the shares they owed). By September 1927, the stock was hovering at around $265. The bull raiders made a profit of more than $10 million, and Cutten and two nominees of the Fisher brothers were elected to the Board of Directors.

It was a stunning coup, one which caught the moneyed establishment completely off guard. These newcomers from Chicago and Detroit, these outsiders, had outwitted Wall Street. Their names were splashed across the financial pages, and their brilliant move on Baldwin quickly became legend.

Cutten claimed to hate the publicity. Yet he also knew that a properly planted story in the press could influence market behaviour, and he was not above promoting a stock when it suited his purposes.

In another move, this time on International Harvester, his shrewd manipulation of the media was evident. Loaded up on shares of the farm machinery manufacturer, Cutten gave an interview in which he

The seven Fisher brothers. Ground-breaking ceremony for the Fisher Building in Detroit, 22 August 1927. From left: Alfred, Lawrence, Charles, Fred, William, Howard, and Edward.

predicted that the stock would go dramatically higher. As reported by the *New York Times* on 15 November 1927, International Harvester soared to a new record of $249, up 9 points on the day that the interview was published.

"The company is constantly expanding its business and profitably," Cutten was quoted as saying. And then the kicker. "I think it quite likely that a price of $300 or $400 a share will be reached."[2] Of course, this fuelled the stock and it took off, reaching $395 within a year.

Cutten wasn't the only one using the media to sell stocks to a gullible public. In fact, many of the large operators on Wall Street employed public relations agents, and some even had "legitimate" reporters on their payroll. David Lion, for example, was the publisher of the *Stock and Bond Reporter*. For publicizing a stock in his tip sheet, he received call options as payment. He also hired other newspaper writers to produce favourable stories, and he employed radio host William McMahon to shill on air. According to later testimony before the US Senate Committee on Banking and Currency,[3] Lion earned half a million dollars on the calls granted to him for his publicity work during the years 1928 and 1930.

John Levenson, a stock operator in the late 1920s, told the same Senate committee that he used Raleigh Curtis of the *New York Daily News* to pump his stocks. Curtis wrote a financial column, under the name of "The Trader," in which he dispensed supposedly impartial and unbiased market commentary. Curtis, however, was on the take. In return for recommending the issues that Levenson was backing, the writer received profits from trading accounts managed by the market hustler.

The Senate inquiry found that publicist A. Newton Plummer spent nearly $300,000 bribing reporters at a number of newspapers to write articles touting his clients' stocks. The rot extended to the *Wall Street Journal*, where columnists who wrote "Broad Street Gossip" and "Abreast of the Market" took payoffs for tipping stocks, the Senate committee reported.

The corruption of the press was widespread, and its duplicity in these schemes ran deep. "In connection with pool operations it was usual and customary for the operators to pay newspaper writers for publicity and propaganda disguised as financial news," the Senate investigation concluded.

Cutten continued to commute daily from his farm, taking the train from Glen Ellyn station to the Loop downtown. He would sit reading his paper, unrecognized by the others, and would chuckle to himself when he overheard nearby passengers discussing his latest moves in the market as though they knew him personally.

He worked from a small, two-room office, Suites 785 and 787, in the Illinois Merchants Bank building (later renamed the Continental Illinois Bank building) at 231 South LaSalle Street near the Board of Trade.[4] The name on the office door was Chicago Perforating Company. He was a director of that company,[5] and perhaps he transacted some minor business on its behalf (it paid him a fee of four thousand dollars in 1929[6]). But the true purpose of the sign was to mislead and misdirect. No one would guess that behind these walls was a trading operation so big and powerful that it was able to rig the market.

Chicago Perforating Company. It was perfect, he thought, particularly in this era of mobsters and running gun battles. If there was one thing he was good at, it was punching holes in his adversaries.

Once a visitor stopped a porter in the hall directly outside the speculator's office. "Can you tell me where I might find Mr. Cutten's place of business?" he asked. With a wink and a smile, the porter replied: "Well boss, if you don't know, I don't either."[7]

Behind the door, Olga Kellenberger sat in a swivel chair at the typewriter. As Cutten's private secretary, she took care of his correspondence and what few records he kept. She answered the phone, giving just the number: "State 2654." It was an important call so she put it through. The fifty-six-year-old speculator in the inner office picked up the receiver. He listened as he watched the stock ticker. Only his eyes moved, darting behind glasses, as he followed the numbers. The gains and losses, the accumulation and distribution of shares, the constant price fluctuations were as tea leaves. From this seemingly random and irrational spew of numbers, the old master was able to see opportunity.

He nodded and hung up. It had been one of his associates. Their stock was off, and it was time to "paint the tape." They would stage a strong rally by coordinating their buying. He picked up another phone, one of several on his desk that connected him to various brokerage firms, and in his sand-paper voice, quietly issued his orders.

While he used many different brokers, his most trusted lieutenant on Wall Street was his younger cousin Ruloff Cutten. A partner in the firm of E.F. Hutton & Co., Ruloff handled the speculator's most important transactions. For Arthur, kinship was a form of insurance. Family members could be counted on for their discretion and loyalty, and in his world, that was everything.

Born 26 March 1896 in San Francisco, Ruloff had been a minor actor on Broadway. Arthur took him under his wing and brought him to Chicago to learn the brokerage business. He was both smart and smooth, and rose quickly through the ranks. By the mid-1920s, Ruloff was successfully established in New York. In addition to serving his famous cousin, he was also a broker for J. Paul Getty.

When the elder Cutten came to Manhattan, he stayed at the Biltmore Hotel or at Ruloff's posh apartment in the Park Lane Hotel (299 Park Avenue). He also kept a suite at the Traymore Hotel in Atlantic City, which he used when he wanted to escape Wall Street but still be close to the action.

While Cutten claimed he acted independently in the market and "played a lone hand," this was not true. On many occasions, he and his close associates synchronized their trading activities to drive up prices, or they participated in a more formal pool operation that bought and sold stock on their behalf.

Montgomery Ward, the mail-order business, was a particular favourite of Cutten's. He knew the president, Theodore Merceles, who tipped him in 1925 that the company planned to open a chain of two hundred department stores across the country. "So it was easy to see that the earnings of the company ought to increase," he observed.[8]

He started buying Monkey Ward, as it was nicknamed, at fifty-six dollars a share and kept buying as the price advanced, accumulating a total of 100,000 shares. Several of his colleagues were also big buyers, and it was rumoured that Cutten was orchestrating their efforts.

The company opened its first freestanding retail outlet in 1926, and within two years had 244 stores in operation. By 1929, it had more than doubled its number of outlets to 531. Profits rose and the stock took off. By the end of 1928, the share price had climbed to $440. Cutten had a paper profit of $36 million on this stock alone.[9]

In October of 1928, Cutten managed a syndicate that purchased a block of stock from Sinclair Consolidated Oil, jacked up the price of the shares through wash trading, and then dumped the securities on the public. Cutten ran the operation from Chicago, and his cousin Ruloff executed the floor trades in New York. David Lion was hired to hype the stock through the publicist's network of crooked journalists.[10]

Within six months, Cutten had driven the share price from thirty dollars to forty-three dollars, making $12 million for the syndicate insiders. The major participants and beneficiaries were Harry Sinclair (head of the oil company), Blair & Co. (Sinclair Consolidated's banker), and of course Cutten himself – each scooping up more than $2.6 million. Chase Securities Corporation (the securities affiliate of Chase National Bank) received $1.7 million, and Shermar Corporation (the personal holding company of Albert Wiggin, then president of Chase Bank) made about $877,000.

And the small investors who believed that buying a "Cutten stock" was a sure thing? By the time a US Senate Committee investigated the scam in 1933 (see chapter 13), the shares were valued at only about eleven dollars.

Simultaneously with the pool in Sinclair Consolidated Oil, Cutten was managing another syndicate formed to sell two large blocks of shares, one in Prairie Oil & Gas Company and another in Prairie Pipe Line Company, which it had purchased from Rockefeller interests for $38 million in late 1928. Again, the major pool participants were: Harry Sinclair, Blair & Co., and Arthur Cutten, with a 21.75 per cent interest each, Chase Securities with a 14.5 per cent interest, and Shermar Corporation with a 7.25 per cent interest.

Through heavy trading on the market, Cutten ran up the prices of the Prairie shares during December 1928 and the first three weeks of January 1929. At the same time, Blair & Co. was busily setting up the Petroleum Corporation of America, the largest investment trust created to date, which would acquire oil company stocks and sell its shares to the public. Similar to a closed-end mutual fund, investment trusts were intended to give small investors a way to participate in a broad number of securities and thereby reduce risk.

Blair and its network of banking houses and security dealers sold more than $100 million of Petroleum Corporation stock to the public at thirty-four dollars per share. Petroleum Corp. then purchased the two blocks of Prairie shares from the syndicate – nicely inflated in price thanks to Cutten's expert manipulation – for $44 million. The syndicate participants made a profit of more than $6 million over a period of seven weeks. Cutten's take was $1.2 million.

Undisclosed to the public, the true purpose of the investment trust was not to manage a diversified portfolio on behalf of small investors but, rather, to create a vehicle for Harry Sinclair to gain control of a key section of the oil industry. A later investigation by the Securities and Exchange Commission concluded: "the formation of Petroleum

Corporation of America created, in effect, a $100-million pool of the public's funds to be employed in furtherance of the plan ... to effect a consolidation of the Prairie companies with Sinclair Consolidated Oil Corporation."[11]

Sinclair Consolidated became Petroleum Corporation's largest stockholder and dominant influence. Elisha Walker, president of Blair & Co. (Sinclair's bankers), was a director of Sinclair Consolidated and chairman of Petroleum Corp. Four other directors of Petroleum Corp. were also associated with Blair & Co., and another eight on the board of Petroleum Corp. (including Cutten) were directors of Sinclair Consolidated.

In March 1932. Sinclair Consolidated, Prairie Oil & Gas, and Prairie Pipe Line Company were consolidated under the name of Consolidated Oil Corporation. By the end of 1935, the Sinclair interests, in part with the aid of Petroleum Corporation of America, had achieved control of a greatly expanded oil system. "The public, which supplied the pool, however, was at no time apprised of this purpose."[12]

The big players all knew each other, and these cozy relationships worked to their advantage. So it was with a pool in Kolster Radio. Formed by George Breen, the operation was set up to sell a block of 250,000 shares of the company. Breen brought in three other partners – Oscar Alexander (his frequent sidekick), Cutten (who had invited Breen into the Sinclair pool), and Lawrence Fisher (one of the brothers involved in the Baldwin Locomotive coup).

Over a six-week period in late 1928, the pool hiked the share price of Kolster from $74 to $96, selling stock at various points on the way up and clearing a profit of $1.3 million for themselves. Again, Ruloff Cutten did the buying and selling on the floor of the New York Stock Exchange and employed David Lion to pitch the stock to an unsuspecting public.[13] Once the pool had liquidated its position, the stock dropped to three dollars. While the small investors and their money were soon parted, the four partners walked away with $337,000 each.

Breen lived in a grand suite at the Sherry-Netherland on Fifth Avenue and summered at the Westchester Country Club in Rye. He helped reorganize the club in 1928 after it ran into financial difficulty, became its president, and persuaded his wealthy friends – including Arthur Cutten, Fred Fisher, Joe Higgins, and John Raskob – to join the exclusive resort. It was a planned community for millionaires and boasted forty-five holes of golf, fifteen tennis courts, three polo fields, a horse racing track, swimming pools, and a brokerage office in the clubhouse.

The club became literally an inner circle of market makers.[14] Members played poker with five thousand dollars on the table and were betting one thousand dollars on a golf game. Their style enabled the club's brokerage office to trade as many as 800,000 shares on a single day.[15]

One of the most glamorous stocks in the late 1920s was Radio Corporation of America (RCA). It was the hot technology company of its day and the most heavily traded issue. Michael Meehan was the specialist for Radio. From Post 12 on the floor, he and his firm handled most of the trading in the shares of the company. He was an Anglo-Irish immigrant who had worked his way up from selling Broadway tickets to running a brokerage firm with eight seats on the NYSE and four hundred employees. He even installed his brokerage operations on ocean liners – the *Berengaria, Leviathan,* and *Bremen* – so wealthy passengers could speculate while making the transatlantic voyage.

With his red hair combed straight back, and a carnation pinned to his lapel, he was probably the most recognized and well-known character on Wall Street. Visitors to the exchange would crowd into the gallery to watch him in action. His exploits were breathlessly reported in the newspapers – for Meehan seemed to be proving that it *was* possible to get rich quick. As Radio moved ever upward, the notion grew that all you had to do was buy a few shares on margin and wealth would follow.

Radio more than quadrupled during 1928, skyrocketing from one hundred dollars to $420 a share. It then sold off in early 1929 before igniting again. During a one-week period in March, Meehan operated a pool in the stock. The participants included John Raskob, William Durant, George Breen, Lawrence Fisher, Joe Higgins, James Riordan, Percy Rockefeller, Walter Chrysler, and Mrs David Sarnoff (the wife of Radio's president).

Meehan wanted Cutten on board and invited him to join the gravy train. But the speculator declined. He had been buying Radio since 1927 and had already established a big position. This presented Meehan with a problem. Cutten held enough stock that, if he decided to unload, he could break the market and ruin the profitability of the pool. They talked it over and came to an agreement. While Cutten would continue as an independent operator, there would be no surprises. The two parties would coordinate their trading in a way that benefited both. It was a happy arrangement.[16]

During that single week in 1929, Meehan boosted the share price of Radio to $570 (adjusted to reflect a stock split). Once he had lured the "little guys" into the stock, he closed out the pool's position and divvied up the proceeds. Meehan's group made a quick $5 million.

In a strange twist of fate, Cutten ended up the owner of a large block of stock in Armour & Co., the giant meatpacking firm, in 1928. This was the company that had thwarted his attempt to corner wheat six years earlier. Cutten had never forgotten the financial pain of that event, and so taking control of the shares settled an old score.

J. Ogden Armour had gone heavily into debt. He had pledged his shares as collateral for loans from the company, and he had been wiped out in a series of disastrous business moves. At his death in August 1927, his estate owed millions. Cutten swooped in and bought the stock. Interestingly, by this time, the president of Armour & Co. was Edson White, Cutten's old friend and roommate from his boarding house days.

Cutten and a group of his associates purchased 951,000 class B shares and 300,000 class A shares for about $10 million. The syndicate later sold, doubling its original investment.

He was the man with the Midas touch. The press hung on his every word and hounded him for his views and stock picks. Rumours of what he was planning, or who he was meeting, drove prices higher.

He was involved in dozens of pools. His name was associated with the biggest advances. He was interested in Loose-Wiles Biscuit Company, Simmons Company, US Cast Iron Pipe, Union Carbide & Carbon

Corp., National Cash Register, American Can, General Motors, F.W. Woolworth & Co., US Steel, and a host of other stocks.

Loose-Wiles was the second largest manufacturer of biscuits and fancy crackers in the country. A group headed by Cutten acquired open market control of the company, buying through the summer of 1928 and propelling the share price from $44 to $89. Mattress manufacturer Simmons was another high flyer. Cutten rode it from $80 to $180. National Cash Register tripled in price. Union Carbide jumped $73 a share. And so on. The wins piled up.

"Just as he thought nothing of dealing in millions of bushels of grain daily ... Cutten has come to plunge just as heavily in stocks," reported the *Chicago Daily Tribune*.[17] The newspaper described him as "the most sensational figure in the present stock market." It informed readers that whenever he arrived on Wall Street, "immediately things began to hum" with reports of new stock deals and sharply higher prices.[18] The *New York Times* observed: "Mr. Cutten may be said to be the leader of the largest and most influential group operating in the market today." It was reported that this syndicate often traded more than a million shares a day on the NYSE.[19] "Mr. Cutten, Chicago capitalist, for many years famous in the grain pits, has been highly successful in his recent stock market operations and is rated as one of the largest holders of securities in this country," the *Tribune* crowed.[20]

On a Thursday evening in April, 1928, a small band of men gathered in a private dining room of the Biltmore Hotel in New York. They arrived separately so as not to attract any attention. They were all friends, they were all multi-millionaires, and they all participated in the same pools.

The dinner was partly a farewell for William Durant, who was sailing to Europe in a few days. The founder of General Motors, Durant had twice lost control of the auto manufacturer and in 1920 had finally been ousted as president of the company. But "Billy," as he was known, was still very wealthy and had made some shrewd bets in the market. A small man who sported an impish grin and grey tufts of hair, he was just as daring as Cutten and just as rich, with paper profits of about $100 million.

The party was also a celebration – a tip of the hat to their good fortune, a salute to their success, a moment to enjoy each other's company and smile with some satisfaction at their immense winnings.

William Durant, founder of General Motors.

The guests included Durant, Fred and Lawrence Fisher, Arthur Cutten and his cousin Ruloff, George Breen, Joe Higgins, Duncan Holmes, and Matthew Brush.

Somehow the *New York Times* had gotten wind of the event, and it published a story the following day.[21] "It was a gathering of men who are leaders of broad speculative activity in the stock market and have all become close friends during the last year or so, all of them working in the same stock market and many times in the same stocks," the

James Riordan.

Times reported. "Possibly the group of men who dined together last night at the Biltmore included the largest individual winners in the present market. At least they have been identified with the stocks which have advanced the furthest and the fastest. Certainly their profits may be measured in millions."

There were others in New York associated with Cutten who worked or consulted with him on various deals. Two are worth mentioning – James Riordan and John Raskob. Both Riordan and Raskob were of Irish-Catholic descent, both had become independently wealthy, and both were friends and supporters of New York governor Al Smith, who was the Democratic presidential candidate in 1928. In contrast, Cutten and most of his colleagues were staunch Republicans and backers of the Hoover-Curtis ticket.

Riordan grew up in lower Manhattan, and paid his way through college with part-time jobs in the city's produce markets. He later organized the United States Trucking Corporation and then went on to found the County Trust Bank. He was a heavy investor in the market, and, through his pals Raskob and Meehan, he got in on some spectacular plays.

Raskob started his career as a secretary to Pierre S. du Pont and worked his way up to become vice-president at the chemical company. He engineered DuPont's control of General Motors, buying out Billy Durant, and was named head of finance at the automaker. In this capacity, he pioneered the industry's use of the instalment plan. He formed the General Motors Acceptance Corporation, which provided long-term financing, making car buying easier for consumers and stimulating sales.

Along the way, Raskob invested his own money in the two companies and made a fortune. He also ran a number of pools, and with du Pont's involvement, it was said that his market dealings were second only to the Cutten-Durant-Fisher operations in size and influence. According to newspaper reports, on some days the two syndicates together accounted for half of all trades on the NYSE.

By 1928, he was chairman of the Democratic National Committee. After Hoover beat Smith in a landslide, Raskob turned his considerable talents to constructing the tallest office tower in the world, the Empire State Building.

Cutten's love of sports, including the Canadian game of hockey, led him into an unusual investment in 1928. Along with a group of other wealthy businessmen he put up money to fund a new arena that would become home to the Chicago Black Hawks. The twenty-thousand-seat stadium at 1800 West Madison Street on the city's West Side was to be the largest in the nation, and the ambitious plans for the venue envisioned major conventions, boxing matches, circuses, ice carnivals, bicycle racing, and more.

The Chicago Stadium Corporation was organized by local sports promoter Patrick "Paddy" Harmon, and, in addition to Cutten, its backers included James Norris (president of Norris Grain Co.), John J. Mitchell (head of Illinois Merchants Trust Co.), Clement Studebaker Jr (president of Illinois Power & Light Corp.), Vincent Bendix (president of Bendix Corp.), attorney Orville Taylor, and a dozen others.

To commemorate the start of construction on 3 October 1928, the directors somehow prevailed upon the reclusive Cutten to take part in a publicity stunt in which he would drive a gold rivet into the first girder of the first floor of the stadium. Much to the speculator's embarrassment and chagrin, the rivet gun failed to work. After repeated attempts, he found himself standing awkwardly before the assembled guests and press until finally, mercifully, he was ushered from the scene.[22]

It should have been an omen for him. The Chicago Stadium was one of his few bad investments. It lost money the first year, and the directors reacted by forcing Harmon from the presidency (he died in an auto accident a few months later). The red ink continued as the company struggled during the depression, and by 1933 it was in receivership. James Norris ended up gaining control of the arena, which cost $7 million to build, for $300,000.[23]

In a nod to Cutten's dominion over the markets, *Time* put him on the cover of its 10 December 1928 edition. Photographed at his Sunny Acres estate, he wore a business suit but also a farmer's tweed cap and was posed – of course – holding a tethered prize bull. "Always a bull, never a bear, Arthur W. Cutten has done more than any other individual to make the overloaded stock ticker lag far behind the market," the magazine observed. "Bull Cutten ranks king of the herd ... [he] has arrived at the position in which any stock that he buys is automatically skyrocketed by his buying it."[24]

Getting up from his walnut desk, Cutten moved across his small, seventh-floor office in Chicago. He walked towards the rear, past the bookcases and filing cabinets, the leather chairs, the davenport, and the smoking stand. When he reached the window, he threw it open. He had two small boxes of cracked corn which he sprinkled on the ledge, and immediately the pigeons gathered and began feeding. It was a long-standing ritual.

He thought of James Patten, his revered mentor, who had just died of pneumonia the previous week. Strangely, Patten's life had ended within twenty-four hours of the closing of the old Board of Trade, where he had operated in the grain pits for forty years.[25] Cutten looked down at the building at the foot of LaSalle Street, now empty and slated for demolition. The final gong had sounded, and operations had been moved to temporary quarters on South Clark Street. A new tower was planned for the old site. When it opened in 1930, it would be Chicago's tallest building and would house a nineteen-thousand-square-foot trading floor.

Cutten shook his head. He didn't care how modern and efficient the new structure would be. When the soot-stained walls of the historic edifice came down, something would be lost. "I loved it," he remembered. "Within its walls I had tasted of triumph and disaster ... it was the finest temple in the land."[26]

And so, a few weeks later, he arranged to buy the two large statues that stood above the main entrance of the old building. It was his way of preserving part of the past from the wrecking crews. The two draped female figures – representing Industry and Agriculture – were twelve feet in height and weighed five and a half tons each. Cutten had them trucked to Sunny Acres. There, the groaning vehicles ground deep ruts into the farm's gravel laneway, the cargo was unloaded, and the stone monsters stored near his wife's garden.

Maud was not amused. She hated the statues, and she would not have them displayed on the property. They remained where they were, prone and covered in dirt, and eventually they were hidden from sight by overgrown thickets.

In contrast to the hidey-hole that served as Cutten's base of operations in Chicago, the business offices maintained by Jesse Livermore – in the Heckscher Building at 730 Fifth Avenue – were the most luxurious in New York.[27] A private express elevator went directly to the penthouse floor. Passing through a metal door, visitors entered an anteroom guarded by Harry Dache, Livermore's bodyguard and chauffeur. He was six-foot-six and a former merchant marine.

Beyond was the massive trading room where half a dozen men on a catwalk posted stock quotations on a green chalkboard. They wore alpaca jackets so they wouldn't smear the chalk symbols, and they listened on headphones to the latest prices being transmitted from the exchange floor. This ensured that Livermore's market information was immediate and avoided the delays of the ticker tape, which could run minutes or even hours late on heavy days. The room featured hand-carved arches, custom bookshelves, and mahogany panels that J.L. had acquired from an old English manor and had shipped to New York. In the centre of the room were eight leather arm chairs around a large conference table.

A team of analysts pored over corporate earnings statements, company press releases, government economic reports, weather maps, trade statistics, and other information, ensuring their boss had the latest intelligence as he traded millions of dollars of stock. Livermore's private office was separated from the trading room by a glass wall so he could follow the action on the board. Three black telephones, direct wires to London, Paris, and Chicago, sat on his desk.

During trading hours, there was absolute silence in the office except for the sounds of the tickers and the chalk on the boards. No one spoke. Livermore would not tolerate any distractions as he concentrated on the fluctuations of the market.

For months now, he had felt that stocks were ridiculously over-bought. He shorted the high flyers, only to watch them continue to climb. Again and again, the Boy Plunger bet against the prevailing mood, certain there would be a reckoning. But none came. Not yet. He lost great sums of money as Cutten, Durant, the Fishers, Raskob and other big operators bulled prices and worked to convince the public that prosperity was here to stay.

The Dow Jones Industrial Average (DJIA) rocketed to three hundred by the end of 1928, gaining 50 per cent for the year and almost doubling since the start of 1927. Huge volumes washed through the exchange, and it was not uncommon to see 7 million shares traded in a single day. The speculative exuberance defied all logic, Livermore insisted, and surely the bubble would burst and the crash would come. He grew angry, frustrated as he continued to lose money on the "wrong" side of the market, and he cursed Cutten and his cronies for kiting prices and selling dreams of easy wealth.

Fisher Brothers: Us Big Boys

Cutten travelled to Detroit to attend a luncheon meeting with the Fisher brothers, which was likely held at the Recess Club. Located on the 11th floor of the Fisher Building, the exclusive club was *the* place to rub shoulders with the city's business and political elite.[28]

Greeting their guest, they waved Cutten into a chair. He sat down and "counted noses. There were only six Fishers. I asked about the seventh," he recalled.

"We'll let him eat with us big boys when he's older," one of them joked.[29]

It was a testament to the close-knit nature of the family. Cutten observed that "they show great consideration for one another." The brothers were inseparable and spent their entire adult lives working together. As a GM president once said: "When one Fisher brother cuts himself shaving, they all bleed."[30]

Their father was a blacksmith and carriage-maker in Norwalk, Ohio. Fred, the eldest son, left school at fourteen and went to work in his father's shop. In 1902, Fred moved to Detroit and found a job as a draughtsman with the C.R. Wilson Company, then the largest maker of horse-drawn carriages in the world and an early manufacturer of bodies for the budding auto industry. Charles, the second eldest, joined Fred in 1904, and for the next few years they learned the trade.

In 1908, Fred and Charles established the Fisher Body Company with a $30,000 loan from their uncle, Albert Fisher, and they began to build auto bodies in a small factory in Detroit. After just a few months, Albert wanted out, and the two boys had to scramble to find financing. Local businessmen Louis and Aaron Mendelssohn provided the capital, becoming shareholders and directors and later multi-millionaires from their investment.

The business struggled at first, but in 1910 it received an order from Cadillac for 150 car bodies to be delivered within a period of a few months. The Fishers were able to meet this deadline because they had tooled their plant to mass produce the wooden components. This eliminated the old carriage-building method of hand-fitting each piece and greatly sped up the manufacturing process.[31]

It was one of many innovations pioneered by the Fishers. Other engineering advances included the development of the "closed body," which allowed motorists to drive throughout the year; the use of insulation to reduce noise and maintain better temperature control; slanted windshields; safety glass; adjustable sun visors; and a unique lacquering process that allowed consumers to choose from a wide variety of car colours.

Within a short period of time, William, Lawrence, Edward, and Alfred joined the business. The youngest, Howard, worked for the company that managed the brothers' investment interests.

Because of its reputation for quality and craftsmanship, Fisher Body grew at an astounding clip. Within eight years of its founding, the company had become the world's largest manufacturer of auto bodies, producing 370,000 a year for customers like Ford, Cadillac, Studebaker, Buick, Oldsmobile, Packard, and Chevrolet.[32]

Wanting to secure its supply of auto bodies, General Motors sought to acquire Fisher Body. GM's president and founder, William Durant, hammered out the deal in September 1919, paying $27.6 million to the Fisher-Mendelssohn group for 60 per cent of their business.

The "Body by Fisher" emblem, displayed on the door sills of GM vehicles, made its first appearance in the early 1920s,[33] and it would remain a symbol of comfort, luxury, and safety for the next seven decades.

In 1926, GM traded 664,720 shares of its own stock, with a market value of $208 million, for the remaining 40 per cent of Fisher Body. The brothers continued to run their business as an in-house division of General Motors, and Fred, Charles, and Lawrence served as directors and officers of GM. Lawrence was also president of Cadillac.

The Fishers were now rich beyond their dreams. Thinking about what to do with all that money, they set up Fisher and Co., an investment organization that they used to carry out their Wall Street operations. They participated in pools with Arthur Cutten and Billy Durant (who had been turfed from GM for a second time in 1920), and they made millions more in the great Bull Market. It seemed they could do no wrong, betting and winning big on such companies as Baldwin Locomotive, Atlantic Richfield Oil, Westinghouse, Montgomery Ward, Radio Corporation of America, International Telephone and Telegraph, Texas Corporation, General Electric, and US Steel.[34]

They moved into upscale mansions that were clustered together in a couple of posh areas of the city. Edward and Charles had estates on West Boston Boulevard, and Fred lived nearby on Arden Park Boulevard. The Palmer Woods area was home to Alfred and William. Howard had a more modest residence on Wildemere Avenue. Lawrence was the exception, building an extravagant villa in Grayhaven.

Two of the Fisher homes were truly exceptional. Charles's sixteen-thousand-square-foot house was the largest in the Boston-Edison District. It featured fourteen bedrooms, fourteen bathrooms, a private chapel, a gymnasium, and a custom-designed pipe organ. Since the house was built during Prohibition, Charles had a pub installed in the basement as well as a vault to protect his private liquor stash.

The most unique estate belonged to Lawrence. The twenty-two-thousand-square-foot, Mediterranean-style villa was built in 1928 for $2.5 million. Located on Lenox Avenue, it backed onto a canal at the mouth of the Detroit River. The flamboyant bachelor was able to drive his yacht right up to the back door.

By the fall of 1929, the brothers' combined assets were said to be approaching $500 million.[35] Investing heavily in the stock market, they had parlayed their payout from GM into a vast fortune. And then along came the October Crash.

Realizing that the sell-off was much more than a temporary correction, they moved quickly to dump their holdings and were able to salvage about $100 million from the wreckage.[36] The boys retreated to their palatial estates where they lived quiet lives, away from the glare of publicity, pursuing their private and philanthropic interests.

The Fisher family ties remained strong, in life and in the hereafter. When their father died in Ohio in 1921, the brothers built a home for their mother on Balmoral Drive in Detroit so she could be close to them. For the next fifteen years until her death, they arranged their schedules so that at least one of them visited her every day. Seven boys, seven days in the week. It all worked out.

Fred died in 1941. The last of the brothers, Edward, died in 1972. All are buried at Holy Sepulchre Cemetery in South-field, Michigan, except Howard, who is interred at St Paul's Cemetery in Norwalk, Ohio.

Ruloff Cutten: A Charmed Life

Ruloff Cutten – those close to him called him "Rully"[37] – was born in San Francisco in 1896. His grandfather and father ran B.M. Atchinson & Co., purveyor of butter, cheese, eggs, hams, bacon, and other produce, a successful business that they operated in the Centre Market.[38]

The Cuttens were wealthy and prominent enough to be written up in the society pages. His mother, Julia (nee Rulofson), enjoyed dances and musical comedies. His father, Joseph, was involved in local politics and was a die-hard Republican.

Ruloff attended local schools and then studied at the San Francisco Art Institute. His true passion, however, was dancing and acting, certainly his mother's influence, and for a time he performed with the stock company of the Alcazar Theatre.[39] He moved to New York where he achieved some minor success as an actor, including a role in the original Broadway production of *Leave It to Jane* at the Longacre Theatre.

After serving briefly with the Naval Reserve during the First World War, he was summoned to Chicago by his cousin Arthur Cutten (technically, they were second cousins once removed). Arthur was already a wealthy commodities speculator, and he was offering Ruloff an opportunity to earn a lot more than a struggling thespian. Rully was given a trainee's position at Clement Curtis & Co., one of several brokerage firms that handled Arthur's trading accounts.

By 1925, he was back in New York. He was married to Ruth Turk,[40] living in a posh apartment, and earning a fat paycheque as a partner in E.F. Hutton & Co.[41] By the time Arthur was ready to shift his attention – and his money – from the Chicago Board of Trade to the Big Board in New York, Ruloff was ready to act as his chief lieutenant.

Arthur usually ran his massive pools from his Chicago office, and he was constantly on the phone to his cousin in New York, issuing his buy and sell orders that Ruloff executed on the NYSE. Rully was involved in the Baldwin Locomotive and Sinclair Consolidated Oil syndicates, among others. He also managed publicity, hiring promoters such as David Lion to generate positive press stories to attract the public into the "hot stocks" that Arthur would then dump at jacked-up prices.

Occasionally, when Arthur had to be in New York, he worked from E.F. Hutton's offices at 61 Broadway. Gerald M. Loeb, senior partner of the firm, recalled the great speculator's visits: "He was a friendly, unassuming personality. Some of [the firm's] clients and board watchers had no idea that the mild-mannered little man who sat and talked with them was one of the market's biggest traders," Loeb wrote.[42]

Ruloff lived well, even after the Crash. He and his wife Ruth maintained a lavish apartment at the Sherry-Netherland hotel which featured eighteenth-century tapestries and museum-quality furnishings. On weekends, they hosted their friends at their 110-acre estate, called Sunset Hall, in Ridgefield, Connecticut. Guests were driven up from New York in the Cuttens' luxury Italian automobile, an Isotta Fraschini. The gossip pages of the newspapers described him as "dark," "suave," and "smooth." She was known for her gracious entertaining and her jewels.[43]

In 1932 and 1933, Ruloff managed a pool in American Commercial Alcohol Corp. It was later revealed that he had received options on shares of the company, while, at the same time, E.F. Hutton was boosting the stock in daily market letters. When called before the Senate Committee hearings conducted by Ferdinand Pecora, he had to acknowledge that this practice was improper since the public was unaware that he had a private interest in the recommended security.

Regardless, this was but a small bump on the road of his charmed life. He was one of the golden boys at E.F. Hutton, and even after his famous cousin died in 1936, Rully continued to make the deals and win over the big customers that helped keep the firm among the top brokerages in the US. He was appointed to the boards of prestigious corporations. J. Paul Getty was one of his clients. He held memberships in the exclusive clubs. He was named one of the best-dressed men in America.[44]

In 1944, he obtained a Nevada divorce from Ruth Turk, and within months married Ruth Lowery, about fifteen years younger than his first wife. Ruloff and the "new" Mrs Cutten resided in New York and spent their winters in California. For a time, they owned a seven-acre estate in Beverley Hills,[45] and later they gravitated to Palm Springs, where they were the toast of the social set. Ruloff died in Los Angeles in 1961 at the age of sixty-five.

William Durant: All In

The founder of General Motors, William Durant was a super salesman who convinced most everyone – himself included – that he had the magic to make dreams come true.

Born in Boston in 1861, he was the product of a doomed union. His mother came from wealth and French ancestry; his father drank and gambled heavily and deserted the family when Billy was a boy.

By 1872, his parents were divorced. Dad disappeared (Billy was later to spend a small fortune in unsuccessful attempts to find him[46]), and Mom and the two kids (Billy and Rosa) went to live with their rich relatives in Flint, Michigan. Billy's maternal grandfather, Henry Howland Crapo (pronounced Cray-poe), had made a fortune in the lumber business and had served as mayor of Flint and governor of Michigan.

Billy dropped out of high school and, at the age of seventeen, took a job at the lumber mill then operated by his uncle. A string of jobs followed. He clerked in a local drugstore, peddled patent medicine, travelled around the county selling cigars, and became a partner in an insurance agency. By the time he was twenty-five, William Durant had a reputation as one of Flint's most enterprising young businessmen.[47]

He married Clara Pitt in 1885. A year later, he acquired rights to a road cart (a horse-drawn, two-wheeled buggy) that had a unique suspension system and, with his friend Josiah Dallas Dort, began production. The Durant-Dort Carriage Company became one of the world's largest manufacturers of these vehicles, with $2 million in sales by 1900. In the midst of all this, he and Clara had two children, Margery and Cliff.

As automobiles proliferated, Durant initially thought these gas-powered machines were smelly, noisy, and dangerous. In 1902 he scolded his daughter for riding in a horseless carriage.

"Margery, how could you – how could you be so foolish to risk your life in one of those things," he admonished.[48]

But he soon changed his tune. He took over management of the financially troubled Buick Motor Car Company in 1904, and with his usual flair for marketing, he increased annual sales from 725 to 8,820 vehicles in four years. Buick was suddenly the best-selling car in the country.[49]

The next two years were frantic ones for Durant, even by his standards. He divorced Clara, and the very next day married Catherine Lederer in a quiet ceremony in New York. She was twenty-two, he was forty-seven. Catherine had been a secretary in his organization, and they had been romantically involved for some time.

On 6 September 1908, he incorporated General Motors. It was his plan to use GM as a multi-brand holding company, selling a variety of vehicles that would appeal to different incomes and tastes. This was in sharp contrast to Henry Ford, who thought his company should be built around one standard car (the Model T), famously saying: "Any customer can have a car painted any color that he wants so long as it is black."

Immediately after its organization, GM took over Buick Motor Company. Then, in rapid succession, Durant added Olds Motor Works Corporation, Oakland Motor Car Company (which later became the Pontiac division), Cadillac Motor Car Co., and many other concerns, including truck and parts supply companies such as Champion Ignition Company (later AC Spark Plug).

In 1909, he almost bought Ford Motor Company. He offered $8 million – $2 million up front, $4 million over three years, and $2 million in GM stock – and Henry Ford agreed to the terms. Durant went to his bankers and, in what can only be described as one of the biggest business blunders of all time, they refused to loan him the money. "We have changed our minds," said the bankers: "The Ford business is not worth that much money."[50]

Known to his employees as "the man" and "the boss," Durant was small of stature (five-feet, eight inches) but of enormous energy. He slept only two or three hours a night, worked eighteen-hour days, and was constantly on the go. "He always had a bag packed," recalled his daughter Margery. "He spent most of his life travelling ... He never planned ahead; he just went."[51]

He played golf and tennis but was good at neither. He much preferred checkers (he even carried around a small checkerboard in his pocket), high-stakes poker, and bridge. He supported Prohibition, though he would have the occasional drink. He loved cigars but later quit, and when he was tempted to smoke he'd take out a stogie and sniff it, which seemed to quell the urge.[52]

By 1910, General Motors owned or controlled more than twenty automobile and accessory companies.[53] But Durant's spending spree had left the operation with a mountain of debt. With GM sliding towards bankruptcy, the banks agreed to step in and rescue the automaker on the condition that Durant give up control. Almost fifty years old, he was out.

Undeterred, confident, always scheming, Durant went right back at it. He would regain control of his "baby" and he would do it in five years. His strategy? Start another car company. He teamed up with Louis Chevrolet, one of his former race car drivers, and they began producing vehicles that were hugely popular with American consumers.

Although the cars were a success, the two partners had a falling out. One story has it that Chevrolet quit because he wanted to manufacture higher-end models while Durant insisted they compete with the lower-priced Ford. Another account suggests that the breakup occurred because Billy was continually harping about Louis's cigarette habit. Reputedly, the race car driver finally had enough and unloaded on the industrialist: "I sold you my car and I sold you my name, but I'm not going to sell myself to you. I'm going to smoke my cigarettes as much as I want. And I'm getting out."[54] Whatever the reason, they parted company and Durant ended up with ownership.

Shrewdly, Durant began to scoop up GM stock by offering to exchange his Chevrolet shares for GM shares. He operated from a suite of rooms in New York's Belmont Hotel, using the phones to buy from brokers as he frantically worked to acquire enough voting stock. By the time of the board meeting in May 1916, he had regained control. With the support of the powerful Du Pont family, which had also been buying up shares of GM, he was back in the driver's seat.

In typical Durant fashion, he celebrated his victory by taking his wife to dinner, not to a fancy restaurant but to a fast-food joint. In the course of the meal, he casually mentioned, "Well, I took General Motors back from the bankers today." Catherine replied, "Oh, Willie. At least we could have gone to the restaurant in the Plaza."[55]

Almost immediately upon his return, Durant started buying again. He merged Chevrolet into GM and then purchased Delco, Frigidaire, and a 60 per cent stake in Fisher Body Company. He operated by the seat of his pants. He made decisions based on instinct and intuition, and he'd do multi-million-dollar deals on the spur of the moment. Alfred P. Sloan Jr, who later became GM president, said that Durant "tried to carry everything in his head. When some thought flashed through his mind, he was disposed to act on it forthwith ... It was just Billy Durant's way."[56]

Mercurial, arbitrary, impulsive, Billy was a perpetual motion machine, happiest when wheeling and dealing and putting together the pieces of his empire. He was an entrepreneur, he lived for the action, and he ran the company by the force of his personality. "He could coax a bird right down out of a tree," said Walter P. Chrysler.[57]

But Billy was not an administrator. He had neither the talent nor the temperament needed to manage such a large, complex corporation, and frankly he had little interest in doing so. He was in too much of a hurry to worry about the details.

When the 1920 recession hit, the lack of organizational discipline again left the company vulnerable. Car sales sagged, the company's finances deteriorated, and GM stock started to nosedive. He tried to support the price by purchasing large blocks of stock on margin, but it was futile. The share price plummeted and Billy lost over $90 million.[58]

Pierre du Pont, by then chairman of GM, agreed to pay off Billy's debts in exchange for control of the company. For a second time, Billy was ousted.

Durant once said: "Forget mistakes. Forget failures. Forget everything except what you're trying to do now and do it."[59] He followed his own advice. With indefatigable optimism and courage, he tried yet another comeback by launching Durant Motors Inc. in 1921.

But his real passion was the stock market. He loved the thrill of great risk and great reward, and now spent almost all of his time speculating in securities. He maintained accounts with at least fifteen brokers and he reportedly paid more than $6 million a year in commission fees. His phone bills were said to be $20,000 a week.[60]

By 1926 he had met Arthur Cutten and the Fisher brothers, and together they were operating one of the most powerful syndicates on Wall Street. They made enormous profits as the market shot upwards on a seemingly endless trajectory, buying massive amounts of stock, pushing prices to stratospheric heights.

In April 1929, Durant met secretly with US president Herbert Hoover. In the dark of night, he arrived in a cab at the White House and was shown to the second-floor study. He was there to warn Hoover that a financial crash was imminent unless the Federal Reserve eased up on its tight money policy. Hoover listened politely but ultimately did nothing.[61] Six months later the stock market tanked.

Billy Durant lost everything. Raymere, his showplace estate in Deal, New Jersey, was sold off. Durant Motors was dissolved. His wife's jewellery was hawked. Declaring bankruptcy in 1936, he listed his liabilities at almost $1 million and his only worldly assets, his clothes, at $250.

By 1940 he was operating a bowling alley and restaurant in Flint. Incredibly, at almost eighty, he planned to open a chain of these establishments, years before McDonalds, that would offer "good food served fast through a window" to accommodate the new nation of motorists he had helped to create. When his wife Catherine asked him why he couldn't just rest, he replied: "We are not given enough time, Mama."[62]

A stroke in 1942 left him unable to work. Destitute, he was supported by friends and old business associates. Always philosophical, he once cheerfully declared: "Money? What is money? It's only a passing pleasure. Human beings are born with nothing, and they leave this world with nothing." He died at his Gramercy Park apartment in New York City on 18 March 1947.

Michael Meehan: At the Rainbow's End

In 1891, when Michael was born, the Meehan family was living in Blackburn, Lancashire, England. His father Thomas worked as a construction labourer. His mother Sarah was employed as a cotton weaver. The town was a major centre of textile manufacturing, but it was an industry in decline. Their prospects unpromising, they packed up their meagre possessions and went in search of a better life.

Sailing on the steamship *Kensington*, the family arrived in Philadelphia in August 1894. By 1900, Thomas and Sarah and their six children (five boys and one girl) had taken up residence in a crowded apartment at 144 West Fifty-Second Street in Manhattan. Thomas had found work as a railroad conductor,[63] and while life was still tough, there was always food on the table and a roof over their heads.

Mike left school after completing grade 8.[64] A series of menial jobs followed, and then, by a stroke of luck, he found work with the United Cigar Company. He was a natural hustler, and he figured out that he could sell a lot more cigars after hours in the theatre district when the shows let out. From there, it was a logical next step to hawk tickets to the Broadway performances, and soon he was working for McBride's Theatre Ticket Agency. He would keep the best seats for his Wall Street customers, and, in return, they would give him stock tips.[65]

He married Elizabeth Higgins, and by 1917 they were living with their two children (two more would follow) in Queen's.[66] Mike earned five thousand dollars a year as manager of the ticket office,[67] and he was also making money in stocks. In fact, he was doing so well as a speculator that he started to think about devoting himself full time to the market. But it entailed risk and there would be no steady salary. He talked it over with his wife, and she encouraged him to take the leap. She reasoned that he'd spend the rest of his life wondering "what if" should he not follow his dreams.[68]

He bought a seat on the Curb Exchange in 1918. Two years later he purchased a seat on the New York Stock Exchange for $90,000 and launched M.J. Meehan and Company. Over the next decade, he became fabulously rich (some estimates put his wealth at more than $40 million). His was truly a Horatio Alger story.

Meehan built one of the most successful brokerage companies in the US, largely by acting as the specialist in the shares of Radio Corporation of America, which meant that much of the trading in RCA was handled by his firm. But he was also operating and participating in pools and taking large positions in a number of high-flying stocks, including Studebaker, Simms Petroleum, Bethlehem Steel, Chrysler, US Steel, National Cash Register, and General Electric.

By 1928, his firm had eight NYSE seats and earned more than fifteen thousand dollars in commissions a day on RCA trading alone. He purchased a beautiful home at 2 East Sixty-Seventh Street directly across from Central Park, where his family and five servants lived (a governess, cook, butler, parlour maid, and chamber maid).[69] He also had a summer residence at Lake Mahopac in upstate New York, and a thirteen-thousand-square-foot winter mansion called Thistle Dhu, with its own eighteen-hole miniature golf course, in Pinehurst, North Carolina.

Part of the Irish Catholic community of New York, he was a huge backer of Governor Al Smith's presidential campaign in 1928 and had close ties to Joe Kennedy, John Raskob, and James Riordan. He became a naturalized US citizen in 1920.[70]

He was short, paunchy, and red-headed. He wore steel-rimmed glasses and a smile for everyone. Known for his generosity, he once gave his employees a full year's salary as a Christmas bonus.[71]

Meehan also had an uncanny ability to sniff out opportunities before anyone else. He recognized the potential of RCA in 1924, far ahead of the herd. He made a small investment in Good Humor Corporation as a favour to a friend and then bought a controlling interest in the ice cream company, which the family held for many years. And in one of his most flamboyant and publicized moves, he installed brokerage offices on three luxury liners so that his rich customers could play the market on the high seas. One of the first to execute an on-board trade was Irving Berlin.[72]

When the Crash came in October 1929, the wealthy passengers on the ocean liner *Berengaria* crowded into the Meehan office. As prices sank, they sent panicked orders to New York to "sell, sell, sell." Cosmetics entrepreneur Helena Rubinstein was there, seated in a leather armchair in the front row. Silent and expressionless, she watched the quotation board as her 50,000 shares of Westinghouse shed $1 million in market value in less than two hours. Finally, she decided to get out and dumped the lot, taking the hit but preserving most of her fortune.[73]

On the floor of the NYSE, Mike was besieged by a crowd desperate to escape the scuttled market as well. He was mobbed by traders with orders to sell RCA at any price. They grabbed and manhandled him, almost tearing the clothes from his back.

When it was over, Mike had lost at least half of his personal wealth, but by some accounts was still worth $20 million.[74] He was famously quoted as saying to one of his managers: "I understand I'm broke. Guess we'd better give all the boys a two weeks' bonus to prove it."[75] He closed down a few branch offices as well as the cruise line operations. But he was far from finished in the market.

In 1931, he ran short-selling operations in Electric Auto-Lite Company and Radio-Keith-Orpheum Corporation. But his real trouble began when the new Securities and Exchange Commission was established in 1934 to regulate the stock market and end manipulative practices. Mike completely ignored the new laws and continued to ply his trading tricks. He drove the price of Bellanca Aircraft from $1.75 to $5.50 a share on the Curb Exchange. As the stock shot upwards, Meehan liquidated his position, producing a healthy profit for his pool participants and leaving the small investors with shares that quickly fell back to earth.

It was a classic Meehan manoeuvre, celebrated in the Roaring Twenties but now illegal. The SEC opened an investigation into trading in Bellanca. Stressed and exhausted, Mike had a breakdown and was sent to the Bloomingdale asylum, an exclusive private hospital in White Plains, New York, in the summer of 1936.[76] According to *Time* magazine, "the SEC challenge had changed him into a tense, excitable, nervous case. He drank frequently and had a tendency toward rambling talk."[77] He stayed in the institution for about a year, restored sufficiently that visitors found him "strutting the grounds, puffing on cigars, and shouting greetings with all his old cockiness and elan."[78]

On 2 August 1937, the SEC expelled Meehan from the stock exchanges and permanently barred him from trading. It could have merely suspended him for a period of time, but it handed out the harshest penalty possible to set an example. Mike became the first broker to be banned by the SEC for rigging stock prices.

For the next ten years, he lived a relatively quiet and still comfortable life, out of the glare of publicity. He died in New York at the age of fifty-six.

George F. Breen: Gun for Hire

When Arthur Cutten needed another operator to help him buy and sell the huge volumes of shares for the various pools he managed, he frequently turned to George Forsythe Breen, one of the wiliest traders on Wall Street.

Breen worked with Cutten on manipulating the share prices of such companies as the Sinclair Consolidated Oil Corporation, netting the pool participants more than $12 million over six months. He and Cutten and two other associates formed a syndicate to bull Kolster Radio from $74 to $96 a share, making $1.3 million for themselves before selling out and leaving the public with stock that collapsed to $3.[79]

For a slice of the profits, Breen hired himself out to corporate insiders and wealthy businessmen who had blocks of stock they wanted to unload at favourable prices. He traded for and participated in various pools, and also speculated on his own. But he was most closely associated with, and famous for, the operations of the Cutten-Durant-Fisher brothers. He was valued and respected for his uncanny "feel" for the market, masterfully timing his transactions, buying on weakness and selling on strength, able to orchestrate prices because he understood the mass psychology of fear and greed.

George Breen acquired his skills at an early age. His father, James A. Breen, was a broker on the Curb Exchange.[80] This was a market where stocks that did not meet the listing requirements of the NYSE were traded, and it literally took place on a street curb. In its earliest years, it was a wild, unregulated market, fertile ground for crooked stock promoters, but it was also a place where one learned quickly or passed into oblivion.

George was born in 1890, the youngest of three children. According to the *New York Times*, he "could read a stock ticker at the age of seven."[81] He got a job as a messenger in the financial district, attended night school, and clerked for a brokerage firm. By 1916, he was a junior partner in James O'Brien & Co. At twenty-six, he was one of the youngest and brightest stars in the business.

It was during this time that he met Michael Meehan and Joseph Higgins, both of whom also worked on the Curb during their early careers. They would become life-long friends and associates, and together would undertake some of the most daring and spectacular plays during the Great Bull Market of the 1920s. Earl Sparling, author of *Mystery Men of Wall Street*, attributes their toughness and success to the training they received "athwart a Wall Street gutter" as they "huckstered like any vegetable peddler in the dust of the street, dodging automobiles to close a deal."[82]

In 1917, George married Margaret Carolyn Schussler.[83] They had two sons – George Jr and Donald – and they retained a staff of live-in servants at their residence in White Plains, New York. By the end of the First World War, George was doing so well in the market that he no longer had to work as a broker. He resigned his Curb membership and devoted his talents to running his own operations.

Breen, like Cutten, was a quiet man. His brown eyes squinted from behind thick spectacles, and his thin lips rarely betrayed any emotion. "I would not advise any man to go into Wall Street unless, as a prime requisite, he has a strong constitution," he once told a reporter.[84] He dressed simply, drove a modest car, and ate at restaurants that provided the best value for money.

Through the heyday of the Roaring Twenties, he maintained offices on an upper floor of the Chase National Bank Building at 20 Pine Street. Behind the doors of an unpretentious waiting room, there was a hubbub of activity as his assistants and clerks tracked the markets, operated some eighty private telephone wires, and kept their boss informed of the

latest financial developments from around the world. Testifying before the Pecora Commission, Breen later acknowledged
that he was heavily engaged in as many as a dozen different
stock plays at any given time during this period.[85]

In 1928, Breen and a number of his associates purchased the
Westchester Country Club in Rye for $5.2 million and turned
it into one of the most exclusive clubs in the US. Members
included Arthur Cutten, the Fisher brothers, Joe Higgins, and
John Raskob. Breen served as president for a number of years
and lived in a handsome summer home on the property.

Even after the Crash, Breen seemed able to maintain his
lavish lifestyle. He commissioned the Consolidated Ship-
building Corporation to build an eighty-one-foot cruiser.
Launched in 1930 and christened *Donmargeo* (named after his
son DONald, his wife MARgaret, and his other son GEOrge),
the yacht allowed him to commute in style between the
American Yacht Club at Rye and the New York Yacht Club's
station at Twenty-Sixth Street and the East River.[86]

After the Second World War, Breen worked primarily
as a securities underwriter. In 1949, he was associated with
a group of New York businessmen in a syndicate known as
Algam Corporation, which purchased the Empire City race
track in Yonkers and converted it to harness racing.[87] As he
neared retirement, European travel and winters in Palm Beach
became more frequent. George Breen died of a heart attack at
his home in New York on 1 July 1957.

CHAPTER EIGHT

Cutten Fields

Dr George Christie, president of the Ontario Agricultural College in Guelph, visited his old friend Arthur Cutten in Chicago in late 1928. Over dinner, the wealthy speculator asked about the college's athletic facilities and was told that OAC had none. Cutten then mused that perhaps he could see his way clear to funding a sports complex that would include a stadium, football and baseball fields, tennis courts, and an eighteen-hole golf course. The facilities would be donated to the city and open to the public, and students and staff of the college would have free use of them. What did he think of the idea? Dr Christie was thrilled, to say the least, and heartily endorsed the plan.

Within weeks, Cutten had his boyhood pal and hometown lawyer Charlie Dunbar quietly buying up parcels of land. The Macdonald Farm, adjacent to the college, was acquired. Along with other properties, a total of 230 acres were assembled.

In addition to the recreational grounds and golf links, Cutten wanted to build a hotel and conference centre that he would also give to the city. In all, he was ready to spend $1 million. The story broke on 20 February 1929. The *Telegram* in Toronto had the scoop. Its front-page headline trumpeted: "ARTHUR CUTTEN GIVES MILLION TO GUELPH." The newspaper even chartered an airplane to fly copies to the Royal City in time for evening readers.

It was an extraordinary gift, and, when announced, it dazzled and delighted the citizens. Cutten was, finally and unquestionably, the favourite son of Guelph.

On Thursday, 11 April, Cutten met with the premier of Ontario, Howard Ferguson, to discuss his plans. Also attending the meeting at the parliament buildings in Toronto were Chick Evans, Charles

Meeting at the Ontario parliament building to discuss plans for Cutten Fields, 11 April 1929. Left to right: Agriculture Minister John Martin, Arthur Cutten, Ontario premier Howard Ferguson, and Dr George Christie of the Ontario Agricultural College.

Dunbar, Dr Christie, Agriculture Minister John Martin, and Lincoln Goldie, who was the provincial secretary and represented the riding in which Guelph was located.

Chick had been invited by Cutten to do the rough layout of the golf course, and he was eager to repay his benefactor for supporting him over the years. "I am up here to lay out the course and do anything I can to make it a success," he told reporters. "I am anxious to help Mr. Cutten put this thing over, in any way I can."[1]

On the following Saturday, the party visited Guelph. Cutten wanted to inspect the site of the golf course, and the politicians wanted a photo op with the famous speculator. Cutten's brothers Harry and Ralph joined the group, and with all of them wearing overshoes and coats, they spent an hour walking about the sodden fields.

Playing to the assembled journalists, the always jocular Premier Ferguson remarked: "Mr. Cutten's generosity is so remarkably large that anything we can do will be but too little." Turning to the home-town hero, he added: "You will make Guelph so attractive you will want to come back here and live." To which Cutten replied: "I wouldn't be surprised."[2]

They came to a summit, and the speculator paused. He looked down on the sloping land that ran to the river. He was lost in thought, no longer hearing the prattle of the politicians or the idle chitchat of his entourage. For a moment, he was transported back a half century. He was Buzz Cutten again. "It doesn't seem long since I was a kid and playing hooky to toboggan down this very hill," he remarked before moving on.[3]

In town, people were all smiles. The press had descended on Guelph, and everyone was talking about Cutten, his visit along with the pre-mier and other dignitaries, and the money he was about to shower on the city.

"He is certainly a great man," a local bus driver told the *Mail and Empire*. "He rides on the bus when he is here. The whole family is like that. Miss Cutten [Lenore] always speaks so friendly. He has made a lot of people rich, they say, because he knows stocks. There is one man here who was earning a salary and he is retired now. They say that Cutten tipped him off one day and he made a pile. Somebody told me it was on General Motors."[4]

Questioned by the media as to his motives for such munificence, Cutten responded with self-deprecating modesty. "I think everybody is making too much of this," he said. "I happen to have the money, Guelph happens to be my old home, the friends of my early youth are here, and I am willing to give the money and the old town is willing to take it. So why should there be all this fuss about it?"[5]

Later, Cutten was strolling down the main street, surrounded by reporters, and an old woman came shuffling by. As she passed, he suddenly realized who she was. Again, a flood of memories filled his mind. "Queen Esther, don't you remember me?" he called after her. She turned. A smile spread slowly across her face. "Shuah. You is Mr Cutten," came the reply. She was the servant who used to do his fam-ily's wash. So long ago. When he was but a boy.[6]

That evening, Arthur retired to Tranquille, his old family home on Stuart Street where his brother Harry and his sister Lenore still lived.

Surveying the lands purchased for the golf club. Left to right: John Martin, minister of agriculture; Howard Ferguson, premier of Ontario; Arthur Cutten; Dr George Christie, president of the Ontario Agricultural College; and Harry Cutten. 12 April 1929.

Sitting in his favourite chair, he listened to his two siblings talking about the exciting events of the day, and he drifted off.

The proposed hotel was to have a combined dining room and auditorium with seating for two thousand people. Cutten felt that it would be a welcome addition to the city and would attract large agricultural conventions. Benjamin Marshall, architect of the Blackstone and Drake Hotels in Chicago, would design the building. And, coincidentally, or not, it was going to be erected on Wyndham Street – just a few blocks from where Cutten's father had operated the disastrous Guelph Banking Company.

But plans for the hotel began to unravel almost immediately. Several merchants had long-term leases on the properties, and once they heard that Cutten was the buyer, they demanded exorbitant payouts to vacate their shops. Cutten declared that he would "not be held up" by the tenants and that he would abandon the project unless they agreed to a reasonable settlement. The discussions broke down, and, true to his word, the tough-minded capitalist turned his back on the development.

The golf course, in contrast, proceeded on schedule. Chick Evans completed the rough layout, and Stanley Thompson was hired to oversee the detailed design. Thompson was one of the world's leading golf course architects, and, over the span of his career, the Canadian designed, remodelled, or constructed some 145 golf courses in Canada, the United States, the Caribbean, and South America. The project was completed in two years, and, according reports, Cutten spent $750,000 on the venture.[7] His wife Maud contributed too, supervising the decoration of the clubhouse's main lounge and ladies' room.

Cutten Fields Golf Club opened on 10 June 1931. The course totalled 6,400 yards and was rated a par 70. At the inaugural ceremonies, Harry Cutten hit the first golf ball, which by all accounts was a decent shot that landed in the centre of the fairway. That evening, Dr Christie presided over a dinner at the OAC's main dining hall, and Edward Johnson, the Guelph-born and now famous tenor with the Metropolitan Opera Company, was the guest speaker.[8]

Some two hundred prominent citizens of Guelph attended the event. Conspicuously absent was Arthur Cutten, the person who had made the golf club possible. Instead, he was in New York where he was being awarded an honorary doctorate by Colgate University (the university's president, George Barton Cutten, was Arthur's second cousin).

Cutten Fields was never deeded to the city as Arthur had intended. The course operated at a loss during its early years, and Guelph mayor Beverly Robson and City Council felt that the taxpayers should not be saddled with the costs, so they declined the offer. Arthur retained title, covered the annual deficits, and appointed his brother-in-law George Foster (Connie Cutten's husband) as the first club manager.

It also came to light (in later legal proceedings) that the golf course cost nowhere near what the newspapers had reported. Arthur Cutten probably spent closer to $175,000 buying the property and making the improvements.[9] Still an impressive expenditure, especially considering that it was made in the midst of the Great Depression, but a far cry from what was implied by all the earlier hype and hoopla.

His largesse had, in the final analysis, been greatly exaggerated. There was no hotel on Wyndham Street. No convention centre. No fabulous sports stadium and complex. And the golf course, which actually cost about a quarter of the touted price, remained in the hands of Cutten.

But the announcement served its purpose. The promise of a million-dollar gift, though it never materialized, bought Cutten a great deal of goodwill. For a time, he was the golden boy whose generosity was unmatched, the native son who was respected and admired by all.

John Raskob, financial executive and businessman for DuPont and General Motors, builder of the Empire State Building, chairman of the Democratic National Committee from 1928 to 1932, and a key supporter of Alfred E. Smith's candidacy for president.

CHAPTER NINE

Cheerleaders

Oh, when you're smiling
When you're smiling
The whole world
Smiles with you

WRITTEN BY LARRY SHAY, MARK FISHER,
AND JOE GOODWIN, 1928. POPULARIZED
BY LOUIS ARMSTRONG, 1929.

The biggest operators on the street knew that stocks would continue to climb only as long as widespread confidence was maintained. For the fabulous bull to keep charging, people had to believe that prosperity was now permanent, that conventional methods of evaluating share prices were no longer valid, and that the greatest financial blunder one could make was to get left behind.

And so men like Cutten, Durant, and Raskob became the cheerleaders of the New Era. In interviews with the press, they talked up the fundamental strengths of the economy and the virtues of investing in America. In private meetings, they encouraged their confreres to speak out in support of easy credit and to promote broader public participation in the markets. And in publicly discussing their own dealings, they expressed an unshakeable confidence in the future. They were always buyers, never sellers, they insisted.

In many ways, Raskob was the ringleader in these efforts to bull the market. In an article in *Ladies' Home Journal* titled "Everybody Ought to Be Rich," Raskob asserted that even small investors could become wealthy by buying stocks. The magazine arrived at newsstands in August 1929, just two months before the crash wiped out the life savings of the vast majority of speculators.[1]

As the market started to wobble and tilt that summer, Cutten gave an interview in which he counselled small investors to "sit tight and not rock the boat." There was no cause for alarm, he advised. The newspaper observed that Cutten's large and enthusiastic speculative following derived considerable satisfaction from this statement.[2]

In another interview, Cutten said there was no end in sight to the current period of prosperity and that even a huge expansion in brokers' loans was nothing to worry about.[3] These utterances assured the masses that the market was safe, that any minor weakness would be met with "organized support," and that the big operators and banks and investment trusts simply wouldn't allow prices to go anywhere but up. For hundreds of thousands of people, Cutten's words signalled that the bull market was guaranteed and that margin buying was the surest way to wealth.

Raskob hosted a luncheon for friends and colleagues at his eighth-floor suite in Carlton House. Attending were Cutten, Durant, Riordan, Percy Rockefeller, the Du Pont brothers, Oris and Mantis van Sweringen, and William Lamb (architect of the Empire State Building, which Raskob was then planning). Ostensibly, the get-together was to update guests on the progress of the office tower. But Raskob's real purpose was to enlist their aid in boosting the market. To protect their own paper profits, he urged them to maintain their long positions and to become more vocal in promoting stock buying to the public. He praised Cutten for his recent positive comments, and others in the room nodded and murmured their appreciation.

On 15 October, days before the slaughter, the *New York Times* quoted Cutten as saying that he was still bullish and that temporary shake-outs did not concern him. "American business is in wonderful shape, and no depression can go very far," he assured readers.[4] Cutten even tried to convince Joseph Kennedy to return to the market. Kennedy had made a small fortune on Wall Street through stock pools, insider trading, and other manipulative practices, and he had then gone on to make millions more by reorganizing several Hollywood studios and merging them into Radio-Keith-Orpheum (RKO).

But by 1928, Kennedy had grown nervous about the overheated market and had cashed out. Now a year later, he was wondering whether he had made a mistake. He had missed a huge run up, and

Pierre du Pont (left) and John Raskob.

perhaps he should jump back in. And so he wanted to meet with Cutten to hear what the famous operator had to say. Raskob, who knew both men, arranged the meeting and invited his friend James Riordan to also attend. On Wednesday, 17 July 1929, the father of future US president John F. Kennedy sat down in a private office at one of the brokerage firms that traded for Cutten.

The meeting was relaxed and informal. First Raskob, then Riordan, and finally Cutten talked, giving their reasons for remaining fully invested and answering questions. At the end, Kennedy thanked them

Joseph P. Kennedy, ca. 1914.

for their time and took his leave. He had other appointments, other operators he wanted to consult. As he made his rounds and chatted with friends, he came to the conclusion that these market insiders were living in a bubble, unable or unwilling to see the bigger picture, and that he had been correct in his assessment that a crash was coming.

According to lore, Kennedy continued on his walk up Wall Street until he reached Number 60, where Pat Bologna operated a shoeshine stand. The nineteen-year-old was reading the *Wall Street Journal.*

Kennedy climbed into the wooden chair. "How's the market, Pat?" he asked.

The shoeblack put aside his newspaper and picked up his brushes. "Booming, Mr. K. Just booming."

"Yeah? You making much?"

"Sure, you wanna tip? Buy oils and rails. They're gonna hit the sky. Had a guy here today with inside knowledge."

"Thank you, Pat."

That evening he told his wife Rose that "a market everyone could play, and a shoeshine boy predict, was no market for Joe Kennedy."[5]

The patriarch of the Kennedy dynasty would come through the crash with his wealth intact and would even make money by shorting various stocks and investing in real estate. In 1934, President Roosevelt would name Kennedy to head up the newly formed Securities and Exchange Commission, reasoning no doubt that it would take a thief to catch the thieves of Wall Street.

As the October reckoning approached, Jesse Livermore was finally having some success in his bear operations. Using his well-known hammering techniques, he sent wave after wave of sell orders into the market, targeting and beating down some of the issues most favoured by Cutten, such as Montgomery Ward, Simmons, US Steel, General Electric, and American and Foreign Power.

"The ascendency of Livermore to the position he once held as the country's leading market operator on the bear side, after several years of eclipse, is one of the most interesting developments in the market," the *New York Times* noted.[6] The newspapers reported that Cutten and Livermore were locked in a titanic struggle for supremacy. The leader of the bulls was trying to organize support for another run, while the bear was trying to maul prices.

Portrait of Arthur Cutten by Frank O. Salisbury, 1929.

The Boy Plunger was incensed at being blamed as the spoiler. He felt the real culprits were the cheerleaders who enticed the public with promises of easy wealth, and on 22 October he issued a written statement to this effect. In part, it read:

> What has happened during the last few weeks is an inevitable result of a long period of continuous, rank manipulation of many stock issues to prices many times their actual worth ... The men who are responsible for bringing about these fictitious prices are the men who are directly responsible for what is happening in the stock market today.[7]

Another portrait of Cutten dates from this time. It was painted by Frank O. Salisbury, a British artist who earned fabulous commissions rendering the likenesses of royalty, presidents and prime ministers, business tycoons, and society elites in London, New York, and Chicago. By this time, Cutten was not only wildly famous for his market exploits, he had also earned the grudging admiration and respect of the corporate bluebloods. He was a director of Baldwin Locomotive, Sinclair Consolidated Oil, Standard Oil of Indiana, Continental Chicago Corporation, and Merchants and Manufacturers Securities Company as well as being a trustee of Northwestern University. Salisbury would have considered Cutten an acceptable subject. The sitting took place at the speculator's city apartment on Lake Shore Drive.

The painting shows Cutten seated in a wooden chair, dressed in a brown suit, one leg crossed over the other, a newspaper in his lap. On close inspection, the newspaper appears to be turned to a page listing securities prices. The subject fixes us with his gaze, the hint of a smile on his thin lips. He is serene, certain, and confident. His grey hair, rimless glasses, and toothbrush moustache assure us. He is a man to be trusted.

Unfortunately, the portrait was unveiled at an exhibition at Chicago's Anderson Galleries on 5 November 1929 – a week after the market meltdown. Instead of affirming that all was right in the world, the painting likely reminded viewers that this was one of the men who had led the grand deception.

John Raskob: Other People's Money

John Jacob Raskob learned at an early age that he would never become rich by earning a salary. The way to true wealth was using "other people's money" and taking calculated risks. The strategy worked beyond his wildest dreams – he built the Empire State Building, engineered the remarkable growth of both the General Motors and DuPont empires, helped shape consumerism and capitalism in twentieth-century America, ran Al Smith's presidential election campaign and chaired the Democratic National Committee, and along the way amassed a personal fortune.

He was born in 1879 in Lockport, New York, of German and Irish descent. His father was a cigar maker, and the staunch Roman Catholic family lived a modestly comfortable life. John delivered newspapers as a boy, graduated from high school, and was taking bookkeeping and stenography classes when his father died in 1898. As the eldest of four children, he felt he had to help out financially, and so he left his studies and entered the workforce.

It was not uncommon then for men to hold secretarial positions, and he worked in this capacity for a number of local firms, starting at five dollars a week. At one point, he was hired by Dominion Iron & Steel Company, and he moved to the coal mining town of Sydney, Nova Scotia. Away from his family for the first time, he discovered there was more to life than mass, duty, and sacrifice.

"He cut loose, at least some. Sydney was a hard-drinking place, and Raskob, a social fellow, learned to consume whiskey and beer, sometimes in tumultuous combination. He had a few raucous nights," says his biographer. "He was on his own and was intent on having fun, but he ran no personal risks and developed no bad habits."[8]

With his usual pluck and audacity, he applied for and landed a job as personal secretary to Pierre S. du Pont. Nine years his senior, du Pont was a brilliant industrialist who had left his family's aging gun powder business and was busy buying up and reorganizing electric street railways. Raskob helped with the negotiations, and du Pont immediately recognized that the younger man had an amazing facility for financial numbers and a talent for spotting corporate value. It was the beginning of a fifty-year friendship and partnership.[9]

In 1902, the two worked together to structure a buyout of the DuPont Company, with Pierre and his two cousins, Coleman and Alfred, gaining control of the business. With loans from his boss, Raskob also invested in the enterprise. Over the next decade, John and Pierre revamped the company, applying modern management practices and new financing schemes that allowed it to consolidate the industry and become the largest explosives conglomerate in America.

Raskob moved his mother and siblings to Wilmington, Delaware – the company's home base – where he had taken up residence. He attended St Mary's Church, and it was there that he became enamoured of the young organist, Helena Springer Green, who played at Sunday services. To arrange an introduction, legend has it that he paid a bribe so he could take the place of the organ-bellows operator in order to sit next to her. True or not as to its origins, the relationship blossomed and John and Helena were married on 18 June 1906. In nine months, the devout couple had the first of their thirteen children, one born almost every year.

During the First World War, the DuPont Company grew at a spectacular rate as the Allies needed vast quantities of its explosive products. The war made the company an industrial giant – and John Raskob very rich. Also during this period, Pierre further solidified his control of the business (buying up Coleman's shares) and, at Raskob's urging, the two of them began to invest in General Motors.

By this time, Raskob had moved his growing family to a country estate named Archmere, outside the city in Claymont, and now he built a new mansion on the site. It featured a two-thousand-foot inner courtyard, covered by a roof of Tiffany-stained glass that could be retracted in the summer, inspired by the Ponce de Leon Hotel, which he and Helena had visited in St Augustine, Florida. The opulent interiors included a panelled library and a music room.[10]

Raskob had been bitten by the automobile craze, and his garage at Archmere was large enough to house eleven cars. He had also identified what he saw as a poorly managed vehicle manufacturer with huge potential, and he convinced the Du Pont family to pour their wartime profits into GM. It was also a smart industrial move as the carmaker would represent a future market for DuPont's chemical, fabric, and paint products.

When Billy Durant, the founder of GM, regained control of the automaker in 1916, it was with the backing of the du Ponts and John Raskob that he was able to reclaim his "baby." Pierre was appointed chairman, and John named to head the finance committee, and they continued to buy GM stock.

Between 1918 and 1920, Raskob created the General Motors Acceptance Corporation, which would allow the burgeoning middle class of America to buy GM cars on credit; he introduced a stock option plan to retain management talent, which the press dubbed the "millionaires' club" because it enriched dozens of GM executives, including Raskob; and he implemented an employee savings plan.

Billy being Billy, of course, went straight back to his old ways of unbridled expansion. Raskob, who was supposed to be exerting greater financial control over the organization, seemed to have fallen under Durant's spell. As fast as Billy built new production facilities and bought up other companies, John was out raising capital and borrowing from the banks to pay for this explosive growth. "Rather than act as brake on Durant's ambitions, Raskob had his foot on the accelerator as well."[11]

In 1920, an economic recession battered GM's sales. Unable to meet its huge debt obligations, the company was teetering on the brink of bankruptcy. Again, it was Raskob who stepped in. With a loan from the House of Morgan as well as the deep pockets of the du Ponts, he rescued the company. And even though he had been a willing accomplice in Billy's crazy spending spree, he showed little remorse when the founder of the company was shoved out the door. Pierre became president, and the du Ponts ended up with a controlling interest in GM.

At the time, GM's corporate offices were located in New York, and Raskob found himself spending longer and longer periods away from his wife and children. He maintained an opulent apartment at the Carlton House, which he shared with Pierre, and he began to explore the nightlife of the city. It was the dawn of the Roaring Twenties, and he had the wealth and connections to mix with high society. He was especially fond of Broadway, and he enjoyed the company of showgirls. He befriended Eddie Dowling, a popular star of the stage. He entertained, and his liquor cabinet was always stocked with the best bootleg booze. He played cards, gambled on golf games, and speculated in the stock market. Distanced from the rigorously conservative world of Wilmington, John Raskob was having fun.

Perhaps to appease his wife for his prolonged absences, he purchased a huge swath of land near Centreville, in rural Queen Anne's County, Maryland, which included the property where she had been born and raised, and he gave Helena free rein to oversee the development of a summer estate. She was delighted and threw herself into the project. It became known as Pioneer Point, and it served as both a summer retreat for the family and a working farm with dairy barns and riding stables.[12]

As the bull market gathered steam in the last half of the 1920s, Raskob made multi-million-dollar bets, either alone or operating with Pierre du Pont and others, speculating in RCA, General Motors, Warner Brothers, Simms Petroleum, Checker Cab, and other hot plays. According to press reports, the Raskob–du Pont group traded as many as 700,000 shares a day and was the second most powerful syndicate on Wall Street after the Cutten-Durant-Fisher operation.[13]

He knew most of the heavy hitters on the Street – among them Arthur Cutten, the Fishers, Mike Meehan, Joe Kennedy, George Breen, Percy Rockefeller – and now his circle expanded to include a group of individuals who operated in the political realm. Because of his Irish-Catholic background, he naturally gravitated to the Democratic Party, which, in New York, was controlled by the Tammany Hall political machine. He was also an ardent anti-Prohibitionist, and these sentiments aligned him with Governor Alfred E. Smith, who was running to be the Democratic candidate in the 1928 presidential election.

After winning the Democratic nomination, Smith selected Raskob to run his election campaign. He also arranged to have Raskob named chairman of the Democratic National Committee.

John hurried to Pioneer Point to share the good news with his family. But instead of a happy celebration, the occasion turned tragic. His second son, Bill, a student at Yale University, was killed in an automobile accident while driving home. Griefstricken, John dealt with the blow the only way he knew how – he returned to New York immediately after the funeral and buried himself in his work. Left without the emotional support she needed, Helena sought solace elsewhere, and soon she and the manager at Pioneer Point, Jack Corcoran, were deeply involved.

The Raskobs maintained their marriage, but it was never again the same. John busied himself with his own pursuits, and Helena and Jack (she was about twenty years older) grew closer as the years went by.[14]

Alfred Sloan, who had become president of GM in 1923, insisted that Raskob could not serve as both the company's finance committee chairman and the head of the DNC. His stated objections were that this dual allegiance would alienate Republican consumers and that it would leave the company vulnerable to antitrust investigation. He demanded that John sever ties to one or the other organization. It is unclear whether Sloan's real motivation might have been his own support for Herbert Hoover or perhaps pressure from the Fisher brothers, who were large shareholders in GM and also big GOP backers. Whatever the rationale, the board backed Sloan, and Raskob was forced to step down from his position at the automaker and devote himself full time to getting Alfred Smith elected.

Raskob took up his new duties with his usual energy and drive, and through his connections to the business and financial elite was able to raise some $6 million for the campaign. It was the first time the DNC had more money to spend than the RNC.[15]

But Smith, the first Catholic to be nominated for president of the United States, could not overcome the combined forces of religious bigotry, the "dry" vote, and the Republican record of prosperity. He was defeated handily by Hoover.

Now with time on his hands, Raskob launched one of his most ambitious projects, one he had been thinking about for a while. He would build the world's tallest building. The undertaking would also allow him to fulfill a promise that he would take care of Al Smith should he lose the election. With the backing of his old friend Pierre du Pont and his own investment of some $2 million, John secured the necessary financing. On 29 August 1929, he announced his intention to erect the Empire State Building and named Smith as president of the new enterprise.

According to one story, Raskob called the building's architect, William Lamb, into his office and, holding an upright pencil, said: "This is what I want the structure to look like, Bill. How high can you make it so it won't fall down?"[16]

As the stock market edged towards the October precipice of 1929, Raskob was also working on a new investment vehicle for the average American. It would allow people to acquire shares in an investment trust by making a small down payment and regular contributions thereafter (much the way GMAC's instalment plan made car buying possible for millions of consumers), and the trust would then professionally manage this pool of money on behalf of its shareholders. It was an early version of today's mutual funds.

To publicize this venture, he had Samuel Crowther, a well-known business writer, prepare an article that was ostensibly based on an interview with Raskob but that, in reality, was a marketing piece touting how the working man could become wealthy by investing a modest amount in the trust. The principles that Raskob laid out were sound, but his timing was awful. The article was published in the August edition of the *Ladies' Home Journal*, two months before stock prices crashed, and it carried the unfortunate title "Everybody Ought to Be Rich."

When the market finally collapsed, "Raskob was mostly on the sidelines. He took a loss in the big selloff but not a bad one," *Forbes* magazine reported.[17]

On St Patrick's Day, 17 March 1930, construction on the Empire State Building got under way. Raskob was in a "mine-is-bigger-than-yours" contest with Walter Chrysler, who was also putting up his own tower about the same time. When the Chrysler skyscraper topped out at 1,046 feet, John simply added more storeys. Completed in May 1931, the 1,250-foot Empire State Building would remain the world's tallest for nearly forty years.

But again, the timing was not favourable. The building attracted few tenants as there was little demand for swanky office space during the Depression. Raskob, Pierre du Pont, and Al Smith took suites on the eightieth floor. The DuPont Company rented offices as well. But the vacancy rate remained over 80 per cent. Jokingly dubbed the "Empty State Building" by New Yorkers, the structure was a money loser for Raskob and his partners well into the 1940s.

(A note in passing. Many are aware that the Empire State Building was used in the 1933 classic film *King Kong*. But few today know that the structure was hit by a B-25 bomber. On 28 July 1945, the twin-engine US Army aircraft was on a routine flight from Bedford, Massachusetts, to Newark, New Jersey, but was lost in a dense fog that hung over New York City that Saturday morning. The pilot had become disoriented and was flying far too low. At approximately 9:45 a.m. the plane crashed into the north side of the tower's seventy-ninth floor, killing the three crewmen and eleven office workers and injuring twenty-six others.[18])

Raskob continued to head the DNC and worked to have Al Smith renominated as the party's presidential candidate in 1932. After Franklin Delano Roosevelt won the nod at the convention in Chicago, John was quickly replaced. It was, he thought, the end of his involvement in politics. He was not in step with the New Dealers, and, following the election, he watched with growing suspicion and scepticism as F.D.R. led the country in a direction that he could not endorse.

As Roosevelt increasingly intervened in the capitalist economy, creating grand public works programs, establishing social welfare systems, and expanding the power and

pervasiveness of the federal government, Raskob concluded
that what he was seeing was an attack on individual freedom
and property rights. And in spite of himself, he was dragged
back into the political fray. Many of his friends and associates
were also murmuring darkly about the destruction of democ-
racy. Together, they resolved to counter these forces through
public education and political action.

They launched the American Liberty League in 1934 and
convinced Raskob to lead the organization. Jouett Shouse,
who had worked with John at the DNC, was named president.
The major backers and supporters included: the du Ponts;
Al Smith; Alfred Sloan at GM; Walter Chrysler; the broker
E.F. Hutton; Howard Pew of Sun Oil Company; John W. Davis,
1924 Democratic presidential candidate and an attorney at
J.P. Morgan; Nathan Miller, a director of US Steel and a one-
time governor of New York; Hal Roach, motion picture pro-
ducer; and Sewell Avery of Montgomery Ward.[19]

The League operated out of the National Press Building
in Washington and, at its peak, had a staff of fifty. Through
speeches, pamphlets, and a syndicated press service, it at-
tempted to sway voters and defeat Roosevelt by castigating
the New Deal as a radical ideology that would shred the Constitution, impoverish citizens, and leave a dangerous dema-
gogue in charge of the country.

But public sentiment during the Dirty Thirties had shifted,
and there was now a great distrust of the financiers and speculators and big businessmen, and it was easy for Roosevelt
and his operatives to portray the League as a group of privileged elites.[20] F.D.R. swept to his second term in 1936, and the
conservative organization lost much of its momentum. It for-
mally dissolved in 1940.

Participating in the League had one major consequence
for Raskob and Pierre du Pont. They were charged with tax
evasion, and both felt they had been targeted by the admin-

istration in Washington for their outspoken opposition to Roosevelt. "One could secure no better illustration of the tyranny which a government bureau can inflict on a citizen," Raskob exclaimed. Pierre remarked that it was "part of a scheme to injure me and to force a compromise of claims in a manner amounting to extortion."[21]

The treasury department charged that they had engaged in a series of "wash trades" in 1929 and 1930 – buying and selling shares between them – to create "losses" that never really occurred and thereby reduce their taxes.

The two men came to an agreement with the Tax Board – paying a total of almost $1.5 million in back taxes.[22] John withdrew once more, this time permanently, from politics.

In his later years, Raskob continued to bestow huge sums to build Catholic schools, hospitals, and churches. He also became interested in mining, ranching, and real estate development. He stayed at the El Mirador when he was in Palm Springs, where he mingled with Hollywood stars, gambled with the rich and glamourous at Bradley's Beach Club in South Florida, and attended opening nights on Broadway. He was having fun again.

Archmere had been sold off in 1932, but John maintained Pioneer Point as a summer home where he enjoyed the company of his children and a growing number of grandchildren. It was here that he died of a heart attack on 15 October 1950 at the age of seventy-one. His wife Helena, released from her vows, married Jack Corcoran in 1952.

(In 1972, the former Soviet Union purchased the mansion and surrounding grounds at Pioneer Point as a vacation place for its embassy personnel in the US. In December 2016, the Obama administration expelled dozens of Russian diplomats and shuttered the property in retaliation for alleged Russian interference in the US election.)

CHAPTER TEN

Carnage

The 1920s had been a period of extraordinary change. America had been transformed, and its citizens now lived far different lives than previous generations. Now, more people resided in cities than in rural areas. Two-thirds of all homes were wired for electricity. Over the decade, the number of cars on the road more than tripled to 23 million. Assembly-line manufacturing churned out goods faster and cheaper, and Americans embraced a new consumerism. They shopped at chain and department stores for vacuum cleaners, refrigerators, washing machines, radios, and a seemingly endless array of new products, and they paid for their purchases on instalment plans.

Credit was easy, and personal debt ballooned. No longer was there any shame in spending beyond one's means: in fact, it was heralded as a sign of confidence in the future progress of the country. Between 1925 and 1929, instalment credit doubled to $3 billion. And because prosperity was considered boundless and inexhaustible during the Roaring Twenties, it only made sense to buy now and pay later.

In accepting the Republican nomination for president in 1928, Herbert Hoover declared "we shall soon with the help of God be in sight of the day when poverty will be banished from this Nation."[1] Cheered by the prospect of continuing abundance, voters swept Hoover to a landslide victory.

Nowhere were the good times more evident than in the securities markets. It was popularly held that the path to riches lay in purchasing the hottest stocks and leveraging one's exposure by buying on margin. This involved putting down only a small percentage of the purchase price (as little as 10 to 20 per cent) and using the shares as collateral for a broker's loan to cover the balance. This greatly enhanced returns when prices rose. It also horribly magnified losses when the market declined.

> The celerity with which margin transactions were arranged and the absence of any scrutiny by the broker of the personal credit of the borrower, encouraged persons in all walks of life to embark upon speculative ventures in which they were doomed by their lack of skill and experience to certain loss. Excited by the vision of quick profits, they assumed margin positions which they had no adequate resources to protect, and when the storm broke they stood helplessly by while securities and savings were washed away in a flood of liquidation.[2]

By late 1929, brokers' loans totalled more than $6 billion. The banks and corporations supplying these funds were getting 10 to 15 per cent on their money, and the nation's capital was being sucked into stock market speculation rather than invested in productive businesses. At the same time, the pools and syndicate operators were driving prices ever higher, and the multitudes were buying like there was no tomorrow. More than one hundred stocks on the NYSE were being manipulated during this period.[3]

The growing popularity of investment trusts also contributed to the instability and volatility of the markets. The public bought these issues on margin, and the trusts themselves owned shares of other leveraged companies. These vehicles were supercharged, skyrocketing on fair winds, nosediving in the slightest turbulence.

The big operators such as Cutten, Durant, the Fisher brothers, and Raskob were often behind these trusts as well. They all had millions in paper profits, but selling their individual stocks would depress prices. By exchanging some of their holdings for trust shares, and then flogging these trust shares to the public (often at a premium to the underlying assets), they could realize even further gains and more easily liquidate their holdings without disturbing the bull market.

During 1928, an estimated 186 investment trusts were organized. In 1929 they were being promoted at the rate of approximately one each business day, and by that autumn their total assets exceeded

$8 billion.[4] After a nine-year run, the market reached a then record high with the Dow Jones Industrial Average (DJIA) hitting 381 on 3 September 1929. Over the next several weeks, prices weakened. By 23 October, the DJIA had declined to 306.

And then the house of cards came tumbling down. The end was sudden, violent, and merciless. In just five trading days, the DJIA plummeted 25 per cent and some $30 billion of stock value evaporated.

24 October, Black Thursday

Waves of sell orders crashed onto the exchange. The nine hundred traders and brokers crowded at the various posts were shouting, waving their hands, trying desperately to unload stocks that were dropping five to ten dollars with each trade.

The clerks inside the horseshoe-shaped trading booths couldn't keep up with the flood of paperwork. No one had ever seen anything like it. Panic gripped the market, and cries of "sell, sell, sell" reverberated through the massive chamber.

Cutten sat at a desk in his broker's office near Wall Street. He was getting prices over a telephone that connected him directly to the exchange floor. With the ticker tape running late, he couldn't rely on it. As he listened on the private wire, the market was in free fall. In just the first two hours, Radio had collapsed 35 per cent and Montgomery Ward had given up 40 per cent.

Yet no emotion showed on his face. Not a frown, nor a grimace, nor any hint of fear. He sat impassively, weighing his options and formulating strategies. He was also getting quotes from the pits in Chicago. Figuring that speculators would dump their grain holdings to meet margin calls (demands from brokerage firms to increase the amount of equity in their trading accounts because of falling securities prices), he issued orders to sell 6 million bushels of wheat. That day, wheat dropped eleven cents a bushel on massive selling.

Winston Churchill happened to be in the visitors' gallery of the New York Stock Exchange that Thursday. Great Britain's former chancellor of the exchequer, he was currently on a lecture tour of the United States, and he had become an enthusiastic market gambler after scoring a few lucky wins. Interestingly, he traded through E.F.

Hutton (one of Cutten's preferred firms), and he had made a tidy profit in Simmons (one of Cutten's favourite stocks).

Fascinated with this quick way to wealth, Churchill had asked to see the exchange first-hand. After an early lunch, he joined a crowd in the second-floor gallery. But rather than the great money-making machinery he had come to see, he witnessed instead a surreal scene on the floor below where traders and brokers were "walking to and fro like a slow-motion picture of a disturbed ant heap."[5]

Whatever paper profits he had simply melted away, and he ended up losing about $75,000 of his original investment.[6] As soon as Churchill left the NYSE that day, exchange officials hurried to close the gallery to the public in a vain attempt to halt the panic.

By noon, the market was down $6 billion. To steady prices, a group of bankers acting in concert began to buy up large blocks of stocks. It was the same strategy used in the panic of 1907 (exactly twenty-two years earlier). With the resources of J.P. Morgan & Co., Chase National Bank, National City Bank and a couple of other financial institutions behind it, the pool purchased some $30 million of key blue-chip issues on the open market. The slide abated and prices began to firm.

A cheer went up on the floor. By the close, half of the morning's losses had been recouped, with the DJIA finishing down 6 points at 300. Disaster had been averted and surely the worst was over.

25 October, Friday

Prices remained firm, and the DJIA actually rose a point to 301. At noon, floor traders mounted a truck at Wall and Broad Streets and cheered. From the White House, President Herbert Hoover issued a statement describing the fundamental business of the nation as being "on a sound and prosperous basis."[7]

26 October, Saturday

There was little change during the short two-hour trading session on Saturday (10:00 a.m. to noon). But now press reports started to circulate alleging that Cutten might have actually profited from the recent market break by shorting the stocks he had been urging others to buy.

The *Toronto Star* accused Cutten of being "the Sampson who pulled down the pillars of the exchange."[8] The *Globe* noted that "a great deal of feeling is being excited by stories that Mr. Cutten, instead of suffering with all the others, had been a bear all along."[9]

Dispatches from his hometown of Guelph estimated that residents there, many of whom had played the market on Cutten's coattails, had lost an estimated $1 million in the past few days.[10] Had their "favourite son" swindled them, just as his father Walter Hoyt had done some forty years earlier?

Secluded in the Traymore Hotel in Atlantic City over the weekend,[11] Cutten called friends, family members, and even the local newspaper in Guelph to assert that he was in no way responsible for the crash and that his own holdings had suffered heavily. He was furious with the newspapers for their spurious claims and attacks on his reputation, and he vehemently denied that he had been engaged in any short selling.

Later he would recount in his memoir: "I was accused of being one of the bears who had started the selling. Nothing could be farther from the truth. I might as accurately be accused of starting an earthquake under my own farm."[12]

28 October, Black Monday

And then on Monday, utter collapse. Great "air pockets" opened up – huge gaps between the ask and bid prices of securities – as sellers overwhelmed the market and buyers retreated. General Electric fell $48 a share, Westinghouse was down $34 a share, US Steel gave up $17.50 per share.

Tens of thousands of margin calls went out to investors. As the value of their stockholdings declined, more collateral was demanded to cover their loans. Already overextended, most were unable to meet the requirements and their accounts were liquidated. Their stocks were dumped on the market, and this depressed prices further.

Clients sat in brokers' offices watching in stunned silence as the ticker tape, lagging far behind, told the grim story. Once again, the bankers huddled to discuss what action they might take. But the rout was too broad and deep, and there was nothing they could do now to halt the devastation.

*Roar of despair. A crowd gathers outside the New York
Stock Exchange during the Crash of 1929.*

The DJIA slid 38 points to 261, down 13 per cent for the day. More than 9 million shares were traded. It took almost three hours after the close of the market for the ticker tape to report the final numbers.

29 October, Black Tuesday

From the opening gong, the exchange floor was in pandemonium. Huge blocks of stock were dumped for whatever price they could bring. Now even the big operators, who a few days before had counted themselves millionaires, were being crushed under the avalanche.

An immense crowd had gathered at the corner of Broad and Wall Streets. People had come to witness the carnage. To quell any possible violence, the police were out in force, stationed on foot and horseback. As the throng grew, a strange roar began to build. It was the sound of fear. Of broken dreams. Of the nightmare to come. The Roaring Twenties were going out in a roar of despair.

Early that morning, Jesse Livermore left his mansion named Evermore in Great Neck, Long Island, and took his chauffeur-driven Rolls into Manhattan. Now ensconced in his opulent offices atop the Hecksher Building, he assembled his staff and issued his orders. As he had over the past few days, he sold short on a massive scale, placing bets against many of the securities that had been promoted by the Cutten syndicate. He shorted Baldwin, Montgomery Ward, Simmons, and Radio. He also hammered away at US Steel, AT&T, General Electric, Westinghouse, American and Foreign Power, and half a dozen other stocks.

By the end of the day, the DJIA had shed another 31 points, closing at 230. A record volume of 16.4 million shares had been traded. And Livermore was millions of dollars richer. The Boy Plunger was back!

The market continued its slide, the DJIA reaching a low for the year of 199 on 13 November. Since the peak in September, shares of Radio were down about 70 per cent, Montgomery Ward and Westinghouse were off 60 per cent, General Motors and General Electric had declined by more than 50 per cent, and US Steel had given up 40 per cent. Things would only get worse.

Hundreds of thousands of speculators, big and small, had been wiped out. Most lost everything. Only a few survived, and Cutten was one of them. According to various accounts, including reports from United Press and the *New York World*,[13] Cutten lost some $50 million – about half of his wealth – in the Crash. This suggests that he was long during the initial stages of the collapse, taking a tremendous beating as a result, and only switched to the bear side and sold short after the October rout.

Still, he was able to retain a chunk of his assets, and, with his usual tenacity, he set about rebuilding his fortune. At the dawn of the Great Depression, the nearly sixty-year-old speculator readied again for combat.

Not everyone was as resilient.

James Riordan, president of the County Trust Company, had been depressed for days. It was said that he had suffered heavy losses in the market. His friend Mike Meehan had persuaded him to invest in Radio, and the stock had tanked. On Friday, 8 November 1929, he removed a .38 calibre revolver from the cashier's desk at the bank and

James Riordan, banker and speculator, died by suicide
8 November 1929 after heavy losses in the market.

took it home with him late that afternoon. He entered the red brick dwelling on West Twelfth Street in Manhattan and proceeded to his bedroom at the rear of the house. He sat at a desk, put the gun to his right temple, and pulled the trigger.

He was found slumped in a chair, life slipping quickly from him. A Catholic priest was summoned, and the banker was given the last rites before he died. As the most prominent financier to die by suicide in the last months of 1929, Riordan became a symbol of the tragedy unfolding across America.

CHAPTER ELEVEN

Holdup on the Gold Coast

On 8 November 1929 – the same date Riordan took his life – Maud Cutten was out on the town with her friends Mabel Martin (her husband Alfred was a retired commodities broker) and Margaret Morton (married to Joy Morton, rural neighbours of the Cuttens). She had invited them to dinner and the opera in the Chicago Loop.

During the performance at the Erlanger Theatre, Mabel noticed an attractive blonde woman who was sitting nearby and watching them closely. Later, while they were waiting outside for the Cutten limo, she again observed the young woman nodding in their direction while talking to two men.

The Pierce Arrow arrived and the three women hopped in. First stop was the Blackstone Hotel, where Margaret was dropped off, and then the limo headed north to the Gold Coast via Lake Shore Drive. At Banks Street it swung west, and then north on State Parkway. About a block from Mabel's home, a sedan came up swiftly from behind, cut sharply in front, and forced them to pull over to the curb. Four men jumped out; one remained at the wheel.

"Police officers!" they shouted, brandishing nickel-plated revolvers. Two pulled the chauffeur James Atkinson from his seat, gripped him by both arms, and marched him around the corner and into some shrubbery where they kept him under guard. Maud knew immediately that they were not cops and that for the second time in seven years she was being robbed.

Two of the thugs stepped to the door of the limo and warned the occupants to remain quiet. "Now ladies, this is a holdup. No screams or we'll shoot you." They got in and sat in the auxiliary seats across from the terrified women. They snatched the rings from their fingers, the strings of pearls from their necks, and the cash from their purses.

Fred Goetz, a.k.a. George "Shotgun" Zeigler.

Mabel thought she recognized the thieves and then realized with a start that they were the men talking with the blonde outside the theatre. The gang had targeted the elderly women as rich and vulnerable – "easy prey" – and had followed them all the way from the Loop.

Repeating their threat to stay silent, they got out and walked to their sedan. A sharp whistle brought the pair guarding the chauffeur on the run. Within seconds, they were back in their vehicle and speeding north. Atkinson ran into the middle of the road, but it was too late for him to make out the licence plate.[1]

After delivering Mabel to her residence, Atkinson drove to the Cuttens' apartment building at 209 Lake Shore Drive. When Maud arrived in the suite, she found Arthur sleeping. She was hysterical.

"I've just been held up," she cried.

"Did they get anything?" her husband asked from his bed.

"A jade ring. They took some of Mabel's jewels."

Arthur put his head back on the pillow. After what he had been going through in the markets for the past week, a four-hundred-dollar ring seemed a trivial matter, certainly nothing to lose sleep over. "But I could not have Mrs. Cutten think I was unsympathetic, so I rubbed the sleep from my eyes and got up to hear about the affair," he recalled.[2]

Cutten didn't want the story to go public, and he asked the police to hush it up. But the details leaked anyway, and soon reporters were knocking on his door. "I don't want to discuss it – what's the use?" he told them. "There'll be a great hue and cry, but the robbers won't likely be caught. If I'd known that the newspapers would get hold of it, I wouldn't even have reported the case."

Indeed, there were no arrests at the time. More than four years later, however, there were reports that Fred Goetz may have been involved. The stories noted that "he [Goetz] was accused of leading the gang that trailed Mrs. Arthur Cutten from a theatre and robbed her of thousands of dollars' worth of jewelry."[3] If true, Maud and Mabel were lucky to have survived the encounter. Goetz, also known as George "Shotgun" Zeigler," was a notorious bank robber, kidnapper, and assassin. Among many other crimes, some reports claimed that he helped Al Capone plan the St Valentine's Day Massacre in which seven members of the rival Bugs Moran gang were executed. Goetz himself was gunned down by a hit squad in 1934.

CHAPTER TWELVE

At the Dawn of the Dirty Thirties

The official opening of the new Chicago Board of Trade building took place on 9 June 1930. Guests gathered in the morning to marvel at the $12 million, forty-four-storey Art Deco edifice, and at 10:00 a.m. President Hoover pressed a button in Washington to signal the start of trading.

Tribune crime reporter Jake Lingle attended the event and then dropped by Cutten's office across the street to say hello. Lingle had been helpful in running down the gang that had looted Sunny Acres, and he and the old speculator had become friends over the years. "He tossed his hand to the level of a smiling face and left," Cutten recalled.[1] It would be a final farewell.

After his visit, the reporter had lunch at the Sherman House Hotel, talked with a few people in the lobby, then walked along Randolph Street and descended into the pedestrian tunnel under Michigan Avenue on his way to catch a train to the racetrack at Washington Park.

In the tunnel, a tall, blond man came up behind him, raised a gun, and fired a single shot into the back of Lingle's head, killing him instantly. The assassin paused over the body. Then he dropped the murder weapon, a .38-calibre revolver, and ran.

Some believed that the hit was in retaliation for Lingle's involvement in bringing Cutten's robbers to justice. Another more probable theory was that the killer had been contracted by North Side gangsters who suspected Lingle was using his influence with the police commissioner to close down their gambling establishments in order to help Capone extend his empire.

The *Chicago Tribune* offered a $25,000 reward for information leading to the conviction of the slayer and launched an investigation. Soon afterwards Leo Vincent Brothers, a St Louis hood, was arrested and

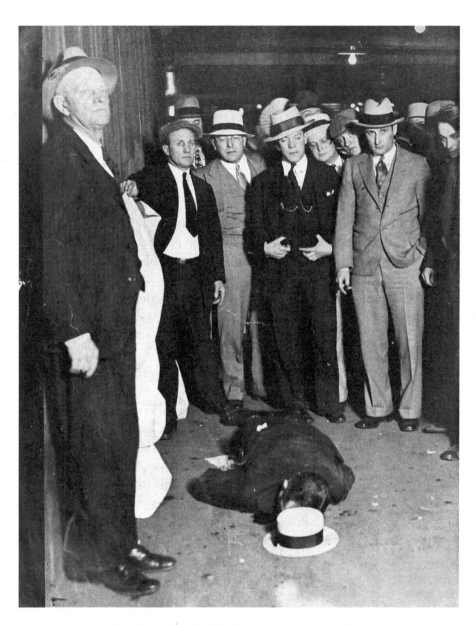

*Jake Lingle, murdered in the pedestrian tunnel under
Michigan Avenue, 9 June 1930.*

Leo Brothers, convicted of killing Jake Lingle.

convicted, and he served eight years in prison. He never revealed who had ordered the murder and went to his grave with the secret.

After the Crash, Cutten returned to the Chicago pits in an effort to rebuild his fortune. But this time he was a bear, short selling wheat and making millions as prices collapsed.[2] Between the beginning of 1930 and the end of 1931, wheat futures prices dropped from $1.34 to 56 cents, and the crafty old speculator profited handsomely.

Of course, it was hugely unpopular, even thought to be unpatriotic, to be betting against the grain markets, and Cutten took extraordinary measures to try to conceal his positions. The Grain Futures Act required him to file reports when he was short or long 500,000 bushels or more in any one wheat contract, and he certainly didn't want the bureaucrats or the public to discover his trading activities.

To get around this problem, he established thirty-five different accounts with eight brokerage firms and split his trades so that no single account ever showed a net position of 500,000 bushels or more. The brokerage houses involved in his scheme were Bartlett Frazier Co., Jackson Bros. Boesel & Co., Clement, Curtis Co., F.B. Keech & Co., James Kidston & Co., C.D. Robbins & Co., Uhlmann Grain Co., and William J. Springer and Company.[3] The accounts were in the names of his relatives and associates, and were usually designated by a number. But Cutten owned or controlled each of the accounts.

Despite his subterfuge, rumours persisted that he was shorting wheat on a massive scale. On 25 February 1930, US secretary of agriculture Arthur Hyde sent Cutten a telegram: It read:

It is reported to me that you have been operating on the bear side of the grain market and that these operations have contributed to the collapse of the market. I have no right or authority to suggest any course to any businessman in his own business, but just in the public interest if you could abandon such a course it would help many thousands of people in a time of distress. If the report is not true, then disregard my anxiety in the matter.

Cutten replied: "Your wire received and your information misleading. I have not been very active in the market."[4]

It was a straight-out lie. In fact, he was short 3,760,000 bushels of wheat that very day. During 1930, he was short 79 per cent of the time he was in the market, and his maximum short position reached 7,525,000 bushels.[5]

While Cutten would go long during brief periods when prices ticked up, he was predominantly a bear. During 1931, when wheat fell below fifty cents before ending the year at fifty-six cents, he was short 89 per cent of the time and his maximum short position was 6,770,000 bushels.

Even Hoover pleaded for the bears (i.e., Cutten) to stop. In a *New York Times* article of 11 July 1931, the president said:

It has come to my attention that certain persons are selling short in our commodity markets, particularly in wheat ...

I refer to a limited number of speculators ... It has but one purpose, and that is to depress prices. It tends to destroy returning
public confidence. The intent is to take a profit from the losses
of other people. Even though the effect may be temporary, it de-
prives many farmers of their rightful income. If these gentlemen
have that sense of patriotism that outruns immediate profit,
and a desire to see their country recover, they will close these
transactions and desist from their manipulations.

Cutten dismissed these entreaties and continued to operate without
regard for the law.

Across America, people drastically curtailed their spending, industrial production fell, investment and construction dried up, one-
quarter of the nation's workers were without jobs, banks foreclosed
on mortgages, and bread lines formed. By 1932, cash wheat had plummeted to forty-three cents. Grain prices didn't even cover the cost of
production, farm income was less than one-third of that earned three
years earlier, and farmers left crops to rot in the fields. Those who
worked and lived on the land felt that the big speculators were driving down crop prices and profiting from the collapse. Resentment and
political unrest grew.

Cutten then made the greatest mistake of his life. For more than
thirty years, he had operated behind the scenes. Other than promoting a particular stock or talking up wheat prices when it suited him,
he had remained a mysterious figure, revealing nothing of his vast
interests or the power he wielded. He had lived by the rule that personal publicity was to be avoided, that public profile only invited un-
wanted attention. He had been able to conduct his business largely
unfettered and unrestrained because he had kept far off the radar of
public scrutiny.

But now, breaking from his own edict, he began to speak out against
government intrusion and what he felt was the erosion of free markets. He launched a concerted attack on the Grain Futures Administration, which regulated the Chicago Board of Trade and other
futures exchanges. He campaigned against its restrictions and reporting requirements, which, he argued, had smothered trading and de-
stroyed the liquidity of the markets. He became "a bitter opponent

of government supervision over grain traders, favouring a wide-open market where anyone with money and a plan of strategy could get plenty of action."[6]

He was also a very vocal critic of the Federal Farm Board, which had been established to stabilize farm prices by buying up grain. But the board's huge purchases – it controlled approximately 250 million bushels of wheat by mid-1931 – had the opposite effect. Its holdings, which hung over the market and which everyone knew eventually had to be sold, further depressed prices. Cutten maintained that politicians and bureaucrats, not speculators, were to blame for the farmers' woes.

He publicly denounced officials of the Farm Board as "bureaucratic lapdogs" who were "growing fat at the farmers' expense."[7] In another interview, he declared: "The Board has almost killed the grain trade. This country was built up by private initiative and not by government bureaus."[8] To make his point, Cutten travelled to Winnipeg, where he purchased a seat on the Winnipeg Grain Exchange, which he stated was "the only free market on the North American continent."[9] (He continued to do the bulk of his trading in Chicago.)

He engaged John Mauff, a former secretary and vice-president of the CBOT, to act as publicity agent and lobbyist in his fight against the Grain Futures Act. On Cutten's behalf, Mauff wrote articles, issued press statements, and conducted meetings with politicians and other officials. (Mauff later had to take Cutten to court for payment. The old speculator claimed he never promised compensation and thought they were working together towards an end they both desired. Mauff sued for $50,000. A jury awarded him $10,000.)

Perhaps Cutten's biggest poke in the eye of government was a series in the weekly magazine *Saturday Evening Post*. Purporting to be his memoirs, the four-part instalment, titled "The Story of a Speculator" and published in late 1932, was a thinly veiled diatribe on the evils of big government and the loss of individual freedom. Cutten commissioned well-known business writer Boyden Sparkes to pen the articles and later self-published the series in a book.

Saturday Evening Post reached a huge audience – its circulation was then more than 2 million copies – and thus Cutten's views and comments were communicated across a wide swath of middle America.

Newly elected President Roosevelt and his New Deal administration took exception to this outspoken critic, and they put him in the crosshairs of their reform agenda.

By abandoning his own rules of absolute secrecy, by becoming a thundering opponent of government, Cutten made himself a target. Why? Perhaps he thought he was above the pettiness of politicians. Maybe he believed that he was on a righteous mission to enlighten the population. Whatever the reason, he committed a grave error, and he would pay for his sin.

The government's first act of retaliation came during the Pecora investigation. Cutten was subpoenaed to testify before the Senate Committee on Banking and Currency in November 1933. Along with other big operators, he was forced to acknowledge that he had manipulated the stock market during the late 1920s through pool operations, secret dealings, and other tricks designed to deceive the public.

It was a most unusual friendship. A quiet, intensely private multi-millionaire who lived a guarded life, and a charming, talkative police reporter who used his street smarts and contacts to make his way.

Cutten first met this "engaging young fellow" at a golf course in Biloxi, Mississippi, in 1926. Lingle was a reporter for the *Chicago Tribune*, and his speech was "rich with unfamiliar yet alluring expressions. The race tracks and gambling houses were as comfortable to him as the Board of Trade to me."[10] Lingle was there with William Russell, who would later become police chief of Chicago, and the three played a round together.

Cutten was a low-handicap golfer, so was Russell. But the rich speculator watched in amazement as the crime reporter teed up a ball, stood back, and then took "two comic little forward steps as he swung his club ... He hit it badly in a curiously inexpert way that betrayed to me that we were kindred spirits, because he, too, had played baseball."

Born in 1891, Alfred "Jake" Philip Lingle was raised in a tough neighbourhood called "the Valley" on Chicago's west side. His family converted from Judaism to Roman Catholicism when he was eight. He dropped out of school after finishing John Calhoun North Elementary and later played semi-pro baseball.

He worked for a while as an office boy with a surgical supply company, and then in 1912 he landed a similar job at the *Tribune*. It wasn't long before he was pounding the streets as a cub reporter. One night he was out covering the police's efforts to clean up the levee district, an area of vice and corruption, and a patrolman ordered him to move on. Lingle objected, and the two got into a shouting match.

When riled, Lingle had a sharp and profane tongue. The enraged cop advanced and was about to use force. Just then police lieutenant William Russell happened by, intervened in the dispute, and saved Lingle from a severe clubbing.[11] The officer and the young newsman became friends, and over the next eighteen years they spent much time attending prize fights, going to the horse races, playing golf, and vacationing together.

During the First World War, Jake used his investigative talents in serving with US naval intelligence. In 1922, he married Helen Sullivan, a childhood friend he had known in grammar school. He had never showed an interest in any other girls and was thirty years old when he finally wedded Helen. They had two children, Dolores and Alfred Jr (nicknamed "Pansy" and "Buddy"), whom Jake adored.

By the mid-1920s, he was a well-respected crime reporter, probably the best in the business. His contacts were extensive. He seemed to know everyone – key politicians, judges and prosecutors, mob bosses and gangsters, industrialists and financiers. He had access to Scarface Al Capone, and interviewed the Big Guy a number of times at his home in Chicago and even at his estate on Palm Island in Miami Beach, Florida.

He never actually wrote his own news copy and never received a byline in the newspaper.[12] He was a "legman." He phoned in whatever scoop he had from tipsters and sources, and an editor at the *Tribune* would type up the article. His value was in ferreting out the facts, working deep in a dangerous and dark world where information was hard to come by and could get people killed.

Because of his connections, Lingle was able to help Cutten in his hunt for the last of the gang members who had raided his country place near Downers Grove. The reporter recommended the best detectives for the case, used his informants to turn up clues, and even went to Cleveland along with Cutten's butler to identify the gang leader, Simon Rosenberg, when he was captured.[13]

Jake visited often with Cutten,[14] driving out to his farm or coming around to his small, unmarked office downtown. They talked about the market, and Jake picked up some valuable stock tips from the speculator. They talked about organized crime, and Arthur sat listening in fascination to his friend's lurid tales. "He spoke as casually of outlaw commerce as I might speak of ordinary business."[15]

By 1930, the newsman was earning sixty-five dollars a week, standard for someone in his position at the time, and yet he seemed to be enjoying a far more affluent lifestyle. He and Helen were living apart because of marital problems – she resided with the children in a rented house on Washington Boulevard,[16] while he had moved into an apartment on the twenty-seventh floor of the Stevens Hotel (then the largest and one of the most opulent hotels in the world). He had also recently purchased a $16,000 cottage in Long Beach, Indiana, where he was looking forward to spending the summer with his family and patching up his relationship with his wife.[17]

He was an avid gambler at the track, never betting less than one hundred dollars on a horse.[18] He vacationed in Havana and rode in a chauffeur-driven Lincoln sedan. He wore a diamond-studded belt buckle, a gift from Capone.

When he was murdered in the pedestrian tunnel beneath Michigan Avenue on his way to play the ponies at Arlington Park on 9 June, he had $1,400 cash in his pocket. The .38-calibre slug dropped him to the ground, face forward and dead instantly, a glowing cigar still clamped in his teeth and the *Racing Form* still clutched in his hands.[19]

Chicagoans were outraged. This time the mob had crossed the line. It was generally assumed that the hit had been ordered to intimidate and silence the press, and such an egregious attack on the foundations of society could not be tolerated. Three city newspapers put up a huge reward totalling $55,000 for information leading to the conviction of the killer, and the *Tribune* launched a massive investigation.

Grief stricken, Commissioner Russell said of his friend: "I was fonder of him than I could be of my own son."[20] Chief of Detectives John Stege lamented: "I haven't much to give, but I would give all I have to be able to arrest the man or men who killed him."[21] Lingle was praised as a fallen hero, a martyr who had lost his life in the war on crime.

His funeral on 12 June was worthy of a head of state. His body lay in a silver-bronze coffin at the home of his wife's parents, and many dignitaries came to pay their respects. A motorcade then proceeded to Garfield Park, where it was joined by marching bands and delegations from the police, fire department, American Legion, and navy. The street was crowded with onlookers, and thousands attended the service at Our Lady of Sorrows Catholic Church. At Mount Carmel Cemetery, a military squad fired its guns in salute and a bugler blew taps at the grave.

Within days, however, the investigation began to reveal that Jake Lingle was not the innocent victim many thought him to be. He had been using his ties to Commissioner Russell to get things done for the mob and had profited handsomely as a result. He was a fixer, an influence peddler.[22] And somewhere along the line he had crossed the wrong men.

As details emerged, people were shocked to learn just how lucrative Lingle's patronage and protection racket had been. He had an annual salary of $3,380, yet he was betting about $15,000 a year at the track. His bank account showed deposits of $60,000 in the thirty months before he was killed.[23] He had been active in the stock market and had several trading accounts, including one he shared with Commissioner Russell. Purchasing stocks favoured by Cutten, such as Simmons,

National Cash Register, Sinclair Oil, and Radio Corporation, he had paper profits of $85,000 before the Crash.

The scandal forced Russell to resign as police commissioner, and he was busted down to the rank of captain. Stege, too, was relieved of command, ousted as head of the detective bureau.

There were many theories about why Lingle had been assassinated. For a time, the authorities considered the possibility that friends or associates of the bandits who had looted Cutten's estate might have wanted revenge for the reporter's involvement in bringing some of the gang members to justice.[24]

Others speculated that the slaying was payback for when Lingle took money to put the fix in for an indoor dog track, failed to deliver, but kept the cash. Or when he demanded a hefty percentage of the take for smoothing the way for a new gambling hall, the mobsters refused to cut him in, and he had the police raid the joint.

A more likely scenario postulated that Bugs Moran's North Side Gang took out Lingle because he had been instrumental in getting Commissioner Russell to crack down on their operations in order to help Capone expand.

In January 1931, acting on a tip, the police arrested a gunman by the name of Leo Vincent Brothers and charged him with Lingle's murder. Convicted at the end of a two-week trial, largely on the basis that he fit the description of the blond gunman in the pedestrian tunnel, he was sentenced to fourteen years. "I can do that standing on my head!" Brothers bragged after the sentence was handed down. He was paroled after eight years. Brothers died of heart disease in 1950, and whatever secrets he had, he took to the grave.

The murder of Jake Lingle – one of the most spectacular in Chicago's gangland history – remains a mystery to this day.

CHAPTER THIRTEEN

The Pecora Commission

9 November 1933, Washington, DC.

"You may proceed, Mr Pecora," directed the chairman of the US Senate Committee on Banking and Currency.[1]

Ferdinand Pecora, the committee's chief counsel, gazed out into the crowded room and announced: "I ask that Mr Arthur W. Cutten be called and sworn."

All eyes shifted to a small grey man making his way to the front. Some four hundred people had jammed into the Senate Caucus Room, every seat was taken, and scores more were standing.

The witness was five feet, eight inches, dressed in a dark suit and crisp white high-collared shirt, lean and wiry despite his sixty-three years of age. He looked more like a school teacher or small-town merchant than a multi-millionaire operator on Wall Street. His neatly parted hair and toothbrush moustache were grey, his face was tanned, and behind rimless glasses his penetrating blue eyes took in everything.

The caucus room was an imposing venue. Measuring fifty-four feet in width by seventy-four feet in length, it featured a dozen marble columns along the walls, three grand windows, and crystal chandeliers hanging from the thirty-five-foot gilded ceiling.

Reporters and photographers jostled for positions. Flashbulbs popped. The man hated having his picture taken, and he moved without a smile or nod to anyone.

"Mr Cutten, will you please stand, hold your right hand, and be sworn," the chairman intoned. "You solemnly swear that the evidence you will give in the proceedings now being investigated by this committee will be the truth, the whole truth, and nothing but the truth. So help you God."

"I do." He settled into a chair, his lawyer Millard Tompkins close by.

US Senate Banking and Currency Committee, Washington, DC, 14 November 1933. Harry F. Sinclair is being sworn in by Senator Duncan Fletcher (committee chairman). Ferdinand Pecora (committee counsel) is seated at the head of the table.

Arrayed around the committee table, the senators sat contemplating this legend who was now before them. They certainly knew of his reputation. He was one of the major manipulators who had fuelled the speculative excesses of the Roaring Twenties, who had run up stock and grain futures prices, made a killing, and then left ruin in his wake when the markets came crashing down. They were fascinated and curious. It didn't seem possible that this dapper little gentleman was at all capable of exercising such immense power and wreaking such havoc on the country.

"What is your business, Mr Cutten?" Pecora began.

The packed Caucus Room grew quiet as the spectators strained to hear. Cutten spoke in a dry, reedy voice, not much above a whisper.

"I have been a broker and grain trader, and have traded in stocks during the last several years."

It was said that Cutten's profits in the grain pits of Chicago and the stock market in New York exceeded $100 million (equivalent to about $1.5 billion today) and that he had stepped from the carnage with at least half his wealth still intact after the Crash of 1929.

"You are a market operator on a pretty large scale, aren't you?" the chief counsel asked.

"Well, I have operated on a pretty large scale for me, yes."

The Senate inquiry had been launched in 1932 to examine the causes of the financial collapse. At first, it had attracted little national attention. Following the election of Franklin D. Roosevelt, however, the new administration wanted to crank up public outrage at the shady practices of Wall Street in order to push through financial reforms. It found the perfect firebrand in Pecora, and he was hired to lead the investigation in early 1933.

Born in Sicily, Pecora was four when his family had immigrated to the United States. They had lived in a cold-water apartment in the Chelsea section of New York, and Ferdinand had grown up scrappy and street smart. He had attended law school, served as assistant district attorney, and had earned a reputation as a hard-nosed prosecutor.[2]

Now he was taking on the financial establishment, and the elite assumed he would be no match for their batteries of lawyers, limitless resources, and privileged status. They were wrong.

Pecora paraded a number of high-profile money men before the committee, using subpoenas to bring them to Washington and dogged determination to uncover abuse and corruption. J.P. "Jack" Morgan Jr, one of the most powerful bankers in the United States, was forced to acknowledge that he and many of his partners had legally avoided paying income taxes during the previous two years. Morgan also revealed that his firm had a list of "preferred" clients who were allowed to buy shares at deeply discounted prices prior to public offerings, including former president Calvin Coolidge; Supreme Court justice Owen Roberts; John J. Raskob, chairman of the Democratic National Committee; and famous aviator Charles Lindbergh.

Charles Mitchell, head of National City Bank, resigned in disgrace after it was learned during the hearings that the bank's investment

Charles "Sunshine Charley" Mitchell, chairman of National City
Bank and its securities affiliate National City Company, 1927.

affiliate had sold millions of dollars of worthless bonds to its customers, manipulated the share price of Anaconda Copper through a huge pool operation, and rewarded its top executives with interest-free loans from the bank. "Sunshine Charley" was also involved in an income tax dodge.

Another respected financier unmasked by the Pecora investigation was Albert Wiggin, former chairman of Chase National Bank. He had been shorting his own bank's stock, selling over forty-two thousand shares in his personal account and making over $4 million as prices plunged in the Crash.

Others were dragged before the Senate committee, and one by one their dealings were exposed. These men all knew each other, and invariably their operations were designed to enrich themselves and their friends at the expense of the public. It was an old boys' club. And they detested this rude intrusion into their affairs. The Senate inquiry, in their view, was a cheap and shabby sideshow. Eventually it would all go away, and they would be able to get back to business.

But Chief Counsel Pecora sensed that the public mood had changed. During the boom days of the 1920s, the wizards of Wall Street were celebrated heroes. They were the high priests of prosperity, and they were making everyone rich.

Now, in the depths of the Great Depression, they were being ridiculed as "banksters." They were seen as having rigged the markets. Now, with more than 80 per cent of the value of securities wiped out, a quarter of the workforce unemployed, breadlines commonplace, and hundreds of thousands of homeless living in shanty towns called "Hoovervilles," there was a deep distrust of the financial establishment. And a growing desire to identify and punish the scoundrels.

So as Pecora eviscerated witness after witness, Americans eagerly followed the proceedings. The newspapers carried daily front-page accounts, and radio stations broadcast the latest shocking exposés.

And now it was Cutten's turn.

"Mr Cutten, according to evidence introduced before this committee," Pecora started to outline the case, "an agreement was entered into between the Sinclair Consolidated Oil Corporation, a New York corporation, and yourself, providing for the sale to you by the corporation of 1,130,000 shares of the capital common stock of that corporation, for a consideration of $30 per share. Do you recall that transaction?"

"Yes, sir."

"Will you tell the committee under what circumstances you entered into that agreement?"

Cutten claimed he had a poor memory. "It is so long ago."

"I know it is so long ago, but it was not an insignificant deal, was it? It was not a trifling thing for you to make a firm commitment to buy over $33 million of the stock, was it?" the chief counsel insisted.

Of course, Cutten's lack of recall was a ruse. The crafty operator had a razor-sharp mind and had always been able to remember even the smallest details of his many complex transactions. Later, his associates would scoff and snicker at his feigned forgetfulness on the stand.

But Pecora pressed on, and slowly, through painstaking interrogation, he was able to extract the facts. In October of 1928, Cutten had agreed to manage a syndicate that would purchase the block of stock from Sinclair Consolidated. The goal was to then sell the shares to the public at a tidy profit.

To ensure success, the master had reached into his usual bag of tricks. First, a press statement was issued announcing that Cutten had formed a group to acquire "a substantial interest" in the common shares of Sinclair Consolidated and that he was to be elected a director of the oil company. This generated a lot of speculative excitement as anything Cutten touched was considered a sure bet.

Next, he quietly set up a second syndicate, a secret trading group, whose sole purpose was to help jack up the price of the shares on the open market. Naturally, this aspect of the operation was never publicly disclosed.

Over a period of six months, Cutten then directed the two syndicates in an elaborate series of transactions. From his office in Chicago, he would phone his cousin Ruloff Cutten, a partner in the brokerage firm E.F. Hutton & Co. in New York, and issue daily instructions on the buying and selling of Sinclair shares.

"How was it intended that the trading account should act?" Pecora asked.

"Well, to keep a market, that we would buy and sell the stock," said the witness.

"What do you mean by 'keeping the market'? Was there not an open public market?"

"Yes."

"Where anybody could go in and buy or sell some stock?"

"Yes, but when the stock was a little weak, on the weak days when the public was selling, we would buy it."

"In order to give support to the market and keep the price up?"

"To support the market at times," Cutten allowed.

This was nowhere near a good enough answer for Pecora. He struck a match and lit his cigar. Blowing smoke, he poked his stogie in Cutten's direction. "The ultimate purpose all the time being to enable your syndicate, your purchasing syndicate, not only to dispose of those shares it bought in the open market to keep up the price, but also to sell at a profit the 1,130,000 shares that it had acquired at $30 a share? Is that right?"

"That is right; yes, sir."

"That is a species of manipulation, is it not, Mr Cutten?"

"I would not call it that, no."

Reviewing the records, Pecora concluded that the two syndicates had been engaged in wash sales – selling to and buying from each other – to give the appearance of a heated market and to lure the public into the stock.

Cutten denied this. "It is often done – the buying and selling of stock."

"What is often done?"

"The buying and selling of stock at the same time."

"For what purpose?"

"I don't know." Hoots of amusement greeted this obvious deceit.

"Did you ever hear the term 'wash sale' used before?"

"I have heard the term used, yes. But it was not done here."

"What does it mean to you?"

"I don't know," Cutten blustered. More guffaws and chortles.

"When you hear the term 'wash sale' used you don't know what it refers to?"

"I have an idea, yes." Now the room erupted with loud and prolonged laughter.

"A man buying from himself and selling to himself is what is meant, isn't it?" Pecora suggested.

"There was nothing of that kind here, I am pretty sure."

Tompkins, Cutten's lawyer, also insisted that "so far as we have been able to check out in our examination, there were no instances where one syndicate sold to the other syndicate."

Senator James Couzens was having none of it. "Well, looking over the exhibits I see there are a number of sales, of purchases and sales that match each other. Mr. Attorney, you cannot convince this sub-committee, or at least so far as I am concerned, with the kind of testimony you are giving, that there were no wash sales or matched sales made in an effort to boost the market. No matter what you may say, Mr Attorney, the subcommittee does not believe that to be a fact."

There was little doubt, however, that the scheme had been a spectacular triumph. By April of 1929, Cutten had driven the share price to over forty-three dollars and unloaded the pool's holdings on an unsuspecting public. The syndicate insiders had netted more than $12 million. The small investors had been left with stock that, by the time of the Senate investigation, was valued at only about eleven dollars a share. Even better for the insiders, Cutten had sold enough of the block of stock to the public before payment was due to the oil company that they hadn't needed to put up a single dollar of their own money.

Senator Duncan Fletcher, the committee chairman, asked incredulously: "You really did not put up any money yourself except what money had come to you from the sale of the stock?"

"Yes," the grey man nodded, "that is right."

The inquiry learned that the major participants in the purchasing syndicate had been Harry Sinclair (head of the oil company), Blair & Co. (Sinclair Consolidated's banker), and, of course, Cutten himself – each making more than $2.6 million. Chase Securities Corporation received $1.7 million, and Albert Wiggin (through his family-owned Shermar Corporation) made about $877,000.

These were explosive revelations, and the room was abuzz. But there was still one more bombshell about to fall. In the course of his testimony, Cutten explained that he had assigned his interest in the Sinclair purchasing pool to a Canadian corporation (Cutten Company Ltd) that was owned by his family members.

In other words, Cutten's share of the spoils (some $1.2 million after paying out his friends Lawrence Fisher, George Breen, and Fred Bartlett) had been transferred to Canada for the benefit of his brothers Lionel, Ralph, and Harry, and his sisters Lenore and Constance. And because Cutten Company had claimed a net loss that year, it had avoided paying any taxes on the Sinclair winnings.

"You turned over your entire interest, did you?"

"Yes," Cutten acknowledged.

"It was a family corporation, was it not?"

"Yes, sir; a family corporation."

"Who owned it? Who owned its stock?"

"My brothers and sisters."

"Why did you turn it over to them?"

After much hounding by the chief counsel, Cutten finally admitted: "I wanted them to make some money, possibly."

"Do you know whether the Cutten Company Limited paid any income tax to the United States Government on the profit derived out of its participation in that syndicate?"

"They said they had not turned in any income tax."

This was the first public disclosure that Cutten had been moving money across the border.

"Are there any further questions by members of the subcommittee?" Senator Fletcher asked. No response. "I believe that is all, then."

Cutten rose from the witness chair and proceeded to the exit. The throng of onlookers parted, watching as he passed.

The Senate inquiry laid bare the financial shenanigans of Wall Street – insider trading, price manipulation, tax dodges, pump and dump operations, the underwriting of shoddy securities, the dissemination of false information through the media, and other abusive practices – all geared towards rewarding the favoured and fleecing the masses.

The revelations stoked public anger and galvanized broad popular support for reform, just as Roosevelt had wanted. The Pecora Commission, as it came to be known, laid the groundwork for major legislation, including the Glass-Steagall Act of 1932, separating commercial and investment banking; the Securities Act of 1933, governing the sale of securities and requiring full and accurate disclosure; and the Securities Exchange Act of 1934, regulating trading in the secondary market and establishing the Securities and Exchange Commission (SEC).

Pecora made the cover of *Time* magazine (12 June 1933) and, at the conclusion of the Senate inquiry, was appointed one of the founding commissioners of the SEC. He was later named a New York State Supreme Court justice.

In 1939, Pecora published a memoir that recounted details of the inquiry and its findings.[3] He wrote: "Had there been full disclosure of what was being done in furtherance of these schemes, they could not long have survived the fierce light of publicity and criticism. Legal chicanery and pitch darkness were the banker's stoutest allies."

About Cutten, he observed that he was "one of the most famous and spectacular market operators in the entire galaxy of the New Era." The Sinclair pool had been a bonanza for its backers because "there was magic – in those days – in the name of Cutten and in the [public's] blind hope that a stock in which he and his associates were interested was going to go up."

Ferdinand Pecora: Against All Odds

According to some accounts, J.P. "Jack" Morgan Jr described him as a "dirty little wop."[4] The elite bankers and money men of Wall Street considered him an intruder, an interloper who didn't belong in their world. *Time* magazine, resorting to the ethnic stereotypes of the day, portrayed him as "the kinky-haired, olive-skinned, jut-jawed lawyer from Manhattan."[5]

Ferdinand Pecora had heard it before, all through his life. The racial denigration. The slurs and insults. The contempt for an Italian immigrant who dared step beyond his station. And when, at the age of fifty-one, he took on the role of chief counsel for the Senate Banking and Currency Committee and encountered the full force of this bigotry, it did not deter him. He would succeed by his sheer brilliance as a lawyer and his understanding of the public mood during the Depression years.

Ferdinand was born on 6 January 1882, in Nicosia, Sicily, to Luigi (Louis) and Rosa Pecora. Louis immigrated in 1883 and, after he had saved enough money, brought his still growing family to New York in 1886. Two boys died within a few years – one succumbed to pneumonia, another drowned in the Hudson River – leaving Ferdinand the eldest son among seven surviving children. They lived in a basement apartment under the L train in Chelsea on the west side of Manhattan. Louis ran a shoe repair shop for a while but then had to find employment in a shoe factory as the Depression worsened.[6]

Always eager to fit in, yearning to be accepted, young "Ferdie" delivered milk and newspapers, was president and valedictorian of his class, and was accepted into St Stephen's College in Annandale, New York, a classic liberal arts college for young men who planned to enter the Episcopal seminary.[7] These plans were cut short, however, when his father was injured at work. Being the eldest male child, Ferdinand was expected to help support the family financially, and he got a job as a law clerk.

It would take many years, but he was finally admitted to the bar in 1911, one of just a handful of first-generation Italian lawyers in the city.[8] By 1918, he was married to Florence Louise Waterman, had a son named Louis, lived in a nice apartment on Riverside Drive, and was assistant district attorney of New York County. He began to make a name for himself by prosecuting and shutting down scores of bucket shops in the city.

He was a top Democratic candidate for district attorney in 1929, but, to his great disappointment, he was not selected. It appeared that he was done with public service. Yet fate had different ideas. The US Senate Banking and Currency Committee had been investigating the causes of the financial collapse, and for almost a year it had been stumbling and bumbling along without any real results. Three chief counsels had come and gone, and it looked as though there was little more to do than to wrap up the proceedings. Pecora was offered the job of writing the final report and, bored in private practice, he jumped at the opportunity.

When he arrived in Washington in January 1933, he discovered that the inquiry had been woefully inadequate. He asked if he could hold an additional month of hearings and was given the go-ahead. Between 21 February and 2 March 1933, he led the committee through the shocking record of abuses perpetrated by the National City Bank (now Citibank) and its investment affiliate. He forced Charles "Sunshine Charley" Mitchell, chairman of the bank and its securities arm, to testify about the millions of dollars of worthless bonds flogged to the public, the interest-free loans given to senior executives, and the manipulation of the bank's own stock, which had been pumped up to almost $580 a share and then had collapsed to $40 by the time of the committee hearings.

Mitchell also admitted to selling his stock in the bank to his wife and later buying back the securities without any money really changing hands in order to create a "loss" and avoid paying income taxes in 1929. In a little more than a week of testimony, the financier – who had dismissed the hearings as a trifling matter that would prove nothing of importance – was a broken man. He resigned from the bank in disgrace. Pecora remembered looking out the window of the Senate Office Building and seeing Mitchell, once surrounded by a battery of lawyers and underlings, now alone and carrying his own suitcase as he made his way to Union Station.

Suddenly, the committee inquiry was the centre of national attention. Pecora made headlines. About to be inaugurated as president after his landslide victory, Franklin Delano Roosevelt urged the new Democratic chairman of the Banking Committee, Senator Duncan Fletcher, to let Pecora continue the probe. It has been reported that F.D.R. met secretly with Pecora and even suggested that the next witness should be Jack Morgan.

And so for the next year, the unlikely chief counsel – the son of a shoemaker, a once poor immigrant who had gone to night school to study law – paraded some of America's most powerful bankers and businessmen before the committee and exposed how they had duped the investing public. Paid $255 a month, Pecora earned less than what his witnesses carried around in pocket change. But he believed in what he was doing, shining a light on the dark practices of Wall Street, and he was exceptionally good at it. The newspaper, radio, and newsreel coverage began referring to the hearings as the "Pecora Commission," and the name stuck.

His small team of investigators were dogged in digging through mountains of corporate records, and Ferdinand never forgot a fact. He worked eighteen- to twenty-hour days and

did his best work at night. He was small and stocky and indefatigable, and his only diversions were occasional rounds of
golf, games of pinochle, ice cream, and large expensive cigars.[9]

He was usually soft-spoken and calm in his cross-
examinations but relentless in getting at the truth. Perhaps
his greatest strength lay in being able to take apart complex,
highly technical financial deals and explain, so that everyone
could understand, how the market manipulators had swindled an unsuspecting public. He became known as "Fighting
Ferdinand" and the "Hellhound of Wall Street." He also had
a flair for the dramatic, and his sense of timing was perfect.
When Morgan first testified, the financier gave an opening
statement in which he said: "I consider the private banker a
national asset and not a national danger."

Without missing a beat, Pecora asked: "What is your business or profession?"

"Private banker," Morgan replied. The audience burst
into laughter.

Senator Carter Glass described the atmosphere of the hearings as a "circus, and the only things lacking now are peanuts
and colored lemonade." During a break the next day, a publicist
for the Ringling Brothers Circus, recognizing a golden opportunity, brought Lya Graf to the Senate room and plopped her
on Morgan's knee before the banker knew what was happen-
ing. She was "the smallest lady in the world," twenty-seven
inches tall, and the perplexed financier could only smile un-
comfortably and wish he were somewhere else as reporters
rushed forward and flashbulbs popped. It was an image that
perfectly symbolized what the American people were learning from the inquiry – the titans pulled the strings and the
little folk danced. The photo was splashed on the front pages
of newspapers across the country.

(Little was heard of Lya Graf again. According to some accounts, her real name was Lia Schwarz. Because of the public-

J.P. "Jack" Morgan Jr, the wealthiest man in America, with Lya Graf, "the smallest lady in the world," at the Senate Banking and Currency Committee inquiry in Washington, DC, 1 June 1933.

ity, she returned to her homeland of Germany seeking a quiet life. She was half Jewish, and in 1937 was arrested by the Nazis as a "useless person." She was later shipped to Auschwitz and put to death.[10])

Under Pecora's questioning, Morgan revealed that the private bank kept a "preferred list" of customers who were offered stock at deeply discounted prices (and who might return a favour when the need arose). This cozy group included former president Calvin Coolidge, Supreme Court Justice Owen Roberts, leading bankers, cabinet officers, even Charles Lindbergh and General John Pershing. The country also learned that the financier paid no income taxes from 1930 to 1932. Although this was because of losses he sustained in the Crash and nothing illegal had transpired, news that one of the wealthiest men in America paid nothing to Uncle Sam while millions went hungry and homeless further outraged the public.

The lords of Wall Street began to complain that the Pecora Commission had gone too far, that it was undermining confidence and becoming a real threat to the stability of the US banking system. F.D.R. replied that they "should have thought of that when they did the things that are being exposed now," and he asked Pecora to keep the heat on. The president needed broad popular support for his financial reforms, and the daily disclosures of fraud, corruption, and abuse coming from the Senate Caucus Room gave him and his administration all the reason they required to regulate the banks and the stock exchanges.

A succession of "banksters," brokers, speculators, and market operators were brought before the commission. While the details varied, the broad themes of their testimony were remarkably similar. They considered themselves above reproach, the rightful masters of the wealth of the country – and if they profited from their labours, well, they were entitled to their rewards because they were serving the greater good.

Albert Wiggin, who had built Chase National Bank into a financial powerhouse, epitomized this condescending, paternalistic attitude. When he appeared before the committee in October 1933, he was a very rich man. He had recently stepped down as chairman and the bank had given him a life pension of $100,000 a year for "his energy, wisdom, vision and character."

But what the bank didn't know, and what Pecora revealed, was that Wiggin had been shorting Chase's stock during the Crash. Even as Chase and a group of other banks tried to shore up the market on Black Thursday by buying millions of dollars' worth of securities on the NYSE, Wiggin was secretly betting that prices would continue to slide. He made $4 million on this operation alone, and, by trading through his personal companies registered in Canada, he avoided income tax.

Wiggin also cut himself in on pools in which the bank's securities arm was participating – including the Sinclair Consolidated Oil pool managed by Arthur Cutten, which put $877,000 in the banker's pocket without any cash outlay upfront.[11] Wiggin also received director's fees for serving on some fifty corporate boards, Chase made loans to his personal companies for trading purposes, and, like Mitchell, he juggled stocks between his wife's and his own accounts.

By the time Cutten appeared before the inquiry, Pecora was as much a household name as the famed market operator. But the chief counsel was now the popular hero, and the man who embodied the golden dreams of the Roaring Twenties was now one of the villains responsible for the bitter realities of the Dirty Thirties. They parried for a while, Cutten claiming his memory and hearing were defective, Pecora patiently repeating his questions, until the facts of the Sinclair Consolidated Oil pool emerged. Although there were no immediate repercussions for the old speculator, his testimony would eventually lead to an investigation by the Bureau of Internal Revenue.

For those who had lost their life savings, their homes, farms, and jobs, the Pecora Commission's revelations were stunning. They were seeing, for the first time, the extent of the

First meeting of the Securities and Exchange Commission, 1934. Standing, left to right: George C. Matthews, Robert F. Healy. Seated, left to right: Ferdinand Pecora, Joseph P. Kennedy, James M. Landis.

corruption, greed, and self-interest that existed among the establishment. The public anger was palpable. Many believed the capitalist system had failed. Some talked openly of revolution.

The inquiry spawned major financial reforms that ultimately helped save capitalism from itself. The Glass-Steagall Act separated commercial and investment banking and established federal deposit insurance. The Securities Act set penalties for filing false information about stock offerings. The Securities Exchange Act created the Securities and Exchange Commission (SEC) to regulate the stock exchanges and protect the public from fraud. And several amendments to the revenue act were introduced to eliminate the tax avoidance loopholes identified during the Senate investigation.

When President Roosevelt announced the new SEC, most observers expected Pecora to be named chairman. Instead, he appointed Joseph Kennedy to head up the agency while Pecora was selected as one of the four other commissioners. There were lots of theories about why the president made this decision – he owed a political debt to Kennedy; he needed to extend an olive branch to Wall Street; or, as F.D.R. himself offered by way of explanation, he felt Kennedy would do a better job of protecting the markets from manipulators because it "takes one to catch one."

Whatever the reason, Ferdinand was once again disappointed. He served on the commission for six months and then accepted an appointment as justice of the New York State Supreme Court, a position he held until 1950. After running unsuccessfully for mayor of New York City, he returned to private practice until his retirement in 1968.

Pecora suffered a heart attack in late 1971 and spent his last days at the Polyclinic Hospital in New York, where he enjoyed regaling the nurses with stories of his exploits as the Hellhound of Wall Street.[12] Against all odds, the little crusader had laid bare the trickery and deception of those who operated behind the walls of high finance.

CHAPTER FOURTEEN

The Last Laugh

Run, run
As fast as you can
You can't catch me
I'm the gingerbread man.

NINETEENTH-CENTURY FOLKTALE

While exposing Cutten's modus operandi and portraying him as a cold-hearted predator, the Pecora Commission inflicted little real damage on the speculator. He could not be sanctioned or charged since Wall Street remained largely unregulated by government. What he did may have been unethical, but it was not illegal. And so Cutten skated.

The feds went looking for other ways to penalize him, to shut him up, to knock this nuisance off his soapbox. The Grain Futures Administration quietly initiated a second investigation, this time into his dealings in the wheat pits. On 9 April 1934, Agriculture Secretary Henry Wallace announced that Cutten was being charged under the Grain Futures Act with concealing his holdings, making false reports, failing to report, and conspiring with brokerage firms to hide his operations in an effort to manipulate prices in 1930 and 1931. The government sought to bar him from trading. Traders at the CBOT rallied to his defence. "This will be a fight and a bitter one," said a grey-haired colleague in the wheat pit.[1]

At the same time, Congress was discussing new legislation to regulate commodity exchanges. The two developments – the revelations about Cutten's secret grain dealings and the loud indignation of the reformers on Capitol Hill – served to convince the public that the big speculators had to be brought to heel.

The politicians continued to ratchet up the rhetoric. Congressman Marvin Jones of Texas proclaimed: "These violent fluctuations had been caused largely by these big traders, such as Arthur Cutten, who are not interested in any way in the maintenance of the market ... I want to see the gambling abolished."[2] Congressman Charles Truax of Ohio declared that Cutten "has ruined more farmers in this country than any other single man. If you could gather together all the bones of the people he has caused to die an economic death, they would form a triumphal arch from Chicago to New York."[3]

The Grain Futures Administration (GFA) commenced hearings in Chicago on 14 May 1934. Cutten did not appear but was represented by his lawyer Orville Taylor. Leo Tierney, counsel for the GFA, laid out the case. During 1930 and 1931, Cutten traded some 116 million bushels of wheat worth about $50 million, yet he failed to report his true position to the authorities. Instead, he split his transactions among many different brokers and accounts in order to hide his activities.

"He was almost always a bear," Tierney noted, although there was no prohibition against short selling. He noted that wheat fell seventy-eight cents a bushel during this period, implying that Cutten was at least partly responsible for the plunging markets and the decimation of farm incomes.

Taylor filed a motion to quash, arguing that the Grain Futures Act was unconstitutional because it deprived his client of the right to a trial by jury. He suggested that the charges, filed three years after the alleged violations, were purposely timed to influence the discussions in Congress over further regulation of grain exchanges.[4] And he accused government of launching the action to silence Cutten and "restrict freedom of speech, the press and the radio."[5]

Final arguments were presented to the Grain Futures Commission in Washington, DC, on Saturday, 12 January 1935. Neatly clad in a brown herringbone suit, Cutten arrived at the Department of Agriculture Building. He and his lawyer were directed to a small conference room where the three commissioners – Agriculture Secretary Wallace, Attorney General Homer Cummings, and Commerce Secretary Daniel Roper – would conduct the proceedings.

Wallace glowered at Cutten. Cutten sat, folded his arms, and watched the Cabinet officers closely. Other than an occasional whisper to his lawyer, he said nothing.

Government counsel Tierney summarized the charges and the evidence, and concluded that "Cutten, the greatest speculator this

Cutten confers with his attorney Orville Taylor at a hearing before the Grain Futures Commission in Washington, DC.

country has ever had, deliberately doctored and juggled reports of his grain trading, which under the act should have been reported. He deliberately masked his market position to conceal his bear position."[6]

Taylor denied all the charges and insisted that this prosecution of his client was unconstitutional. At the close of two hours of argument, the commission announced that it was taking the case under advisement and would return a decision in the near future. Cutten left for Chicago.

A month later, newspaper headlines around the country announced "Cutten Barred from Trading." The commission found that he had violated the Grain Futures Act by concealing his operations in an attempt to manipulate grain prices, and it prohibited him from trading for two years beginning 1 March 1935.

Taylor issued a statement on behalf of Cutten:

The finding of the Commission is outrageous and manifestly inequitable. Because of his prominence, Mr. Cutten has been singled out, prosecuted, and made the object of an unconstitutional penalty. With the Secretary of Agriculture acting in the capacities of prosecutor and judge, it has always been manifest that, if the ends of justice are to be served, they will only be served at the hands of the courts. This case illustrates the degree to which constitutional rights and privileges are being jeopardized by the star chamber bureaucratic commission type of judicial procedure which the department of agriculture, seemingly with the approval of the present administration, is inflicting on our people.

Taylor immediately filed a petition in the US Circuit Court of Appeals in Chicago, and, on 28 February, the court stayed the commission's order until the appeal could be heard. Cutten didn't lose a day of his market privileges and was free to continue to trade.

In November, the appeals court announced its decision, reversing the order of the Grain Futures Commission. The court found that the act was worded in such a way that it applied only when a trader "[was] violating" the law, not when violations had occurred in the past. Cutten got off on a technicality, but it was a victory nonetheless.

Licking its wounds, the government appealed to the Supreme Court. Bent on putting Cutten out of business, it also commenced a third assault. The Bureau of Internal Revenue began going over his books.

Exhausted, harassed by the unending government probes, Cutten was stricken with double pneumonia in November 1935. He was admitted to Passavant Memorial Hospital in Chicago. After a month's treatment he was released, and he went to recuperate at the nearby Drake Hotel.

Then, on 26 December, he suffered a heart attack. He was placed under an oxygen tent and assigned constant nursing care. There was little that could be done for him. The medical experts judged his heart condition to be incurable.[7]

Propped up in bed, Cutten signed his last will and testament. Witnessed by his personal physician Dr Arthur Byfield, the attending nurse Ethel Dickinson, and his lawyer Orville Taylor, it was a simple, single-page will:

I, Arthur W. Cutten, hereby give, devise, and bequeath all my property, real, personal and mixed, of whatsoever character and wheresoever situated, to my beloved wife, Maud Cutten.
I hereby revoke all other wills by me made.
I appoint my said wife, Maud Cutten, executrix of this my last will without bond.
IN WINESS WHEREOF, I hereunder set my hand and seal, this 15th day of January, in the Year of Our Lord, One Thousand Nine Hundred and Thirty-Six.

Arthur W. Cutten

On 3 March 1936, US district attorney Michael Igoe announced that a federal grand jury would be asked to indict Cutten on charges of income tax evasion. The government claimed that he owed $1.2 million in taxes and penalties for the years 1929, 1930, and 1933.

In an attempt to reach a settlement, the government sent an assistant deputy attorney to Chicago to confer with Cutten's lawyers. But the old speculator, stubborn and cantankerous as ever, instructed his attorneys to reject all offers of compromise. He felt that his reputation was being impugned, and he resolved to stand firm. He would fight this assault, just as he had the other attacks by his enemies in Washington.

Cutten was indicted twice – first for income tax evasion in 1929 and then for attempting to evade payments in 1930 and 1933 – and both times deputy marshals showed up at his bedside at the Drake Hotel and served him with a warrant. Cutten signed a $35,000 surety bond guaranteeing his appearance in court.

Then some good news amidst all the troubles. On 18 May 1936, the US Supreme Court ruled in Cutten's favour and against the Grain Futures Commission. In a unanimous decision written by Justice Louis Brandeis, the court affirmed that the commission was empowered "to act only against persons who are presently committing offenses; and that consequently it had no authority to deny to [Cutten] trading

Edgewater Beach Hotel, Cutten's last residence.

privileges for violations committed more than two years prior to the institution of the proceedings against him."[8]

It was a huge win for Cutten, but it came at an enormous cost. The old market operator was now so physically and emotionally spent that his doctor ordered him to give up all business activities. In a statement to the press, his wife Maud announced: "Mr Cutten will never be strong enough again to take up trading. He is just going to rest from now on."[9]

His victory in the Supreme Court spurred Congress to pass the Commodity Exchange Act just one month later. Replacing the Grain Futures Act of 1922, the new law closed the loophole that had allowed Cutten to escape prosecution, strengthened provisions against manipulation, and gave government the authority to limit the size of speculative positions by individual traders or those acting in concert with each other. It marked the end of an era. The curtain was coming down on the wild west of LaSalle Street.

In June he was moved to the Edgewater Beach Hotel, and a slight improvement in his health allowed him to take short daily walks. As he ambled about the grounds, he must have recalled the golden days when – a quarter century earlier – he and his friend Chick Evans had played golf not far from here.

In his bed at the Edgewater, Arthur reached for the phone and called his brother Lionel in Toronto.[10] It was 9:00 p.m., Tuesday, 23 June.

"How are you feeling?" Lionel asked.

"First rate," came the answer.

They talked about the recent Joe Louis–Max Schmeling fight, lamenting the outcome (Schmeling won by a knockout in round twelve) and expressing the hope that the American boxer would get another shot at the German. They caught up on family matters, said goodnight, and rang off. Five hours later, Arthur's heart gave out. With Maud beside him, he exhaled his last breath and slipped away.

Even before Cutten was buried, the US government – cheated by his death because it could no longer pursue criminal charges of tax evasion – made it clear that it wasn't giving up. Assistant District Attorney Carl R. Perkins stated that, while the indictments would be dismissed, the government had every intention of proceeding with a civil suit to collect the back taxes and penalties from the estate.[11]

On Thursday, 25 June, friends and business associates gathered at St James's Episcopal Church in Chicago to remember the "Wheat King." The Board of Trade sent a delegation of nineteen members, including Allan Clement, Arthur Lindley, and Harry Lobdell. Ruloff Cutten, Arthur's cousin and chief stock trader, travelled from New York to attend.[12]

That evening, his casket was loaded onto a train. Arthur was on the last journey home to Guelph. Maud accompanied the body, escorted by George Barton Cutten of Colgate University, Ruloff Cutten, Arthur Lindley, and Harry Ash.

A private service was held the next day at Tranquille, the old family home, followed by a large funeral at St George's Anglican Church. The rich and powerful were jammed into the pews – Hugh Guthrie, former federal minister of justice; J.B. Bickell, mining magnate; Bert Collyer,

Maud Cutten with unidentified relative as she leaves St James' Episcopal Church in Chicago following her husband's funeral.

publisher; Toronto mayor William Robbins; Frank Hughes, former justice of the Supreme Court of Canada; and Justice Nicol Jeffrey of the Supreme Court of Ontario were but a few of the dignitaries.

As the silver-grey casket was borne down the aisle, the bells of the carillon – which Arthur had donated years earlier – rang out "Nearer, My God, to Thee." At the front of the church, family members and close friends sat together, some quietly weeping. Among them were Robert Torrance and Charlie Dunbar, who had known Buzz since boyhood and had remained pals with him all these years.

The crowd poured out to watch as the casket was taken to the hearse. A long line of cars formed and, under police escort, made its way to Woodlawn Cemetery. Passing through the iron gates, also a gift from Cutten, the procession came to a stop at the huge granite obelisk that marked the family plot.

A brief burial service was conducted, and then the casket was slowly lowered into the earth. The sun shone fitfully through clouds. The crowd melted away, and workmen started to close the grave. In a few days, stone masons would arrive to add Arthur's name on the monument.

A month after his death, it was learned that Cutten – who once controlled a fortune estimated at $100 million – left assets worth only about $350,000.

Dwight Green, attorney for the American National Bank & Trust Company of Chicago, the administrator of the estate, made the stunning revelation before the Probate Court of Cook County.[13] It had been widely assumed that the speculator, after sustaining heavy losses during the Crash, had been able to salvage some $50 million from the wreckage and had then gone on to rebuild his wealth.

Had Cutten been wiped out? Had he gone bust, like his father?

If not, where was the money?

Rumours began to circulate that he had secretly transferred millions of dollars to family members in Canada. The family denied these claims. But for many observers, including government officials on both sides of the border, it was simply inconceivable that a man such as Cutten – the boldest, shrewdest, and biggest operator in the markets – could have lost so badly at his own game.

"We suspected most of the Cutten estate might be in Canada," said US assistant attorney Carl Perkins in a press interview.[14] And so the treasury department filed civil claims against the estate for $1.2 million in unpaid income taxes and penalties in the expectation that the missing money would be found.

Then a stunning revelation. Harry Ash, former assistant attorney general of Illinois, filed a petition with the probate court declaring that Cutten had indeed been sending funds out of the country for years.[15] According to his statement, he had been personally acquainted with Cutten and had partnered with him in various trading activities.

Ash maintained that Cutten told him a year before he died that he had retained most of his wealth and that he had transferred the greater part of it to his brothers and sisters. "The decedent [Cutten] informed the petitioner [Ash] that he was transferring virtually all of his assets out of his name and was sending a great many of them out of the country and placing them in the names of various members of his family and various corporations located in Canada," the petition claimed.

Ash was seeking $158,000 from the estate (he claimed that was the amount owing to him from the sale of securities to Cutten), and he was asking the court to launch ancillary proceedings in other jurisdictions to uncover the hidden assets. The court agreed to his request and authorized a search. During the summer of 1937, a team of investigators made several trips to Toronto, Guelph, New York, and Washington, and met with more than a dozen individuals. Those interviewed included Lionel, Ralph, and Harry Cutten; their cousin Edward Chudleigh, who was also Ralph's business partner; George Foster, Connie Cutten's husband and manager of the Cutten Fields Golf Club; Cutten's attorneys Walter Buckingham and Angus Dunbar (Charlie Dunbar's son); and the investment bankers and heads of brokerage firms who did business with Cutten. Investigators also travelled to Ridgefield, Connecticut, where they interviewed Ruloff Cutten at his estate.

In addition, the Ontario government opened up its own probe into Cutten's financial affairs to determine if succession duties were owed.

J. Douglas Peck, a lawyer with the provincial treasury department and controller of revenue, supervised the initiative.

The various inquiries discovered a number of things. First, Arthur had remained the beneficial owner of Cutten Fields, and, therefore, the golf course was part of the estate. However, the administrator estimated its current market value at only $10,000 to $15,000.[16] Second, at the time of his death, Arthur had a beneficial interest in most of the shares of Cutten Company Ltd (this was disputed by the family), which held assets worth about $70,000. Third, title to Sunny Acres, the farm near Downers Grove, had been transferred to Maud several years earlier, and, therefore, the US tax authorities could not get their hands on the proceeds of its sale. And, fourth, one of the brothers (likely Lionel) admitted that he had received funds from Arthur, but he claimed receipt of only $60,000 and agreed to pay 20 per cent in duties to the Ontario Treasury. "None of the others [in the family] indicated any desire to settle with us," noted an internal government memo.[17]

No great stash had been found, no secret accounts containing millions had been uncovered. The search would continue, incredibly, for another decade, but never did any real evidence surface proving conclusively that Cutten had spirited vast sums out of the country.

Yet there were hints, glimpses of what he may have been up to, going back years.

One scheme involved Jackson Brothers & Company, a Chicago brokerage firm where Cutten maintained numerous trading accounts. According to court documents, it was alleged that the firm transferred money to a bank in Toronto and that the bank used these funds to purchase Canadian bonds, which it placed in a safety deposit box. The bank then received instructions from Jackson Bros. to release the bonds to Arthur's brother Lionel, and Lionel came to the bank and withdrew the certificates. It was claimed that at least $2 million came across the border in this manner from 1917 to 1922.[18]

Another $500,000 was deposited in a trust fund created by Cutten on 2 January 1918 to provide life incomes to six family members.[19] Cutten Company Ltd provided another means to transfer money and avoid taxes. Arthur claimed the Canadian company was owned by his family members, but in reality he controlled it (according to documents filed with the probate court) and used it as a vehicle to move funds into Canada.[20]

Consider, too, that Cutten knew, likely for years, that he had an incurable heart condition. He had visited a medical specialist as early as 1925.[21] Keenly aware of his mortality, he would have settled his affairs far in advance of his death. His simple, one-page will also suggests that his assets had already been dispersed well before he died.

The probate court finally closed the estate on 23 December 1948. The US Bureau of Internal Revenue received a cheque for $333,464, which was all that it would ever collect against its claim of $1.2 million.[22]

Arthur Cutten would have loved how the final act played out.

He had walked away unscathed from the Senate investigation into his manipulative stock market practices; he had won against the Grain Futures Commission in the US Supreme Court and kept his trading privileges; and now it appeared that he may have eluded the taxman and had the last laugh at the government's expense.

Somewhere, he was smiling.

CHAPTER FIFTEEN

Final Threads

What became of those who, having been central or pivotal characters in Cutten's life, outlived the old speculator? Some kept their wealth, some lost everything in the Great Depression. Some remained in the public spotlight, some faded quietly into obscurity, and some went out in a last blaze of notoriety. Of those not dealt with earlier, here is a brief roundup.

Jesse Livermore

By the mid-1930s, J.L. was flat broke again. He had lost the great fortune he had made in the Crash, he was $2 million in debt, and he had to file for bankruptcy once more.

He was married to his third wife, Harriet Metz Noble (whom he nicknamed "Nina"). He drank more heavily than ever and suffered from bouts of depression. He tried repeatedly to make a comeback but failed. The new Securities Exchange Act had fundamentally changed the game, and the Boy Plunger could no longer play fast and loose. Unable to manipulate the market as he had in the past, he knew he would never recover.

On 27 November 1940, Jesse and Harriet were at his favourite watering hole, the Stork Club. A photographer asked if he could take their picture. Jesse nodded his consent, then added in a faraway voice: "But it's the last picture you'll take because tomorrow I'm going away for a long, long time."[1]

The next day, he went to drink alone at the Sherry-Netherland Hotel. He sat near the bar and finished off two old-fashioneds. He then walked to the cloakroom, pulled out a .32-calibre pistol, and shot himself behind his ear. He died instantly.

Jesse Livermore and his wife Harriet Metz Noble at the Stork Club in New York, 27 November 1940. The next day, he shot and killed himself.

Police found a suicide note of eight small handwritten pages in Livermore's personal, leather-bound notebook. "My dear Nina," it read. "Can't help it. Things have been bad with me. I am tired of fighting. Can't carry on any longer. This is the only way out. I am unworthy of your love. I am a failure. I am truly sorry, but this is the only way out for me. Love Laurie."[2]

He left two sons, Jesse Jr and Paul. Jesse Jr took his own life in 1976.

Maud Boomer Cutten (Wife)

Other than a widow's award of $25,000 to support her in her "customary style" for the first year after her husband's death, Maud received nothing from Arthur's estate. (She did receive $145,000 from the sale of the farm, which was in her name.) Yet she continued to live in style at the Drake Hotel, was regularly mentioned in the society pages of the *Chicago Tribune*, attended dinner parties and the theatre with her friends, and remained active in raising money for various children's charities.

Maud died at Presbyterian–St Luke's hospital in Chicago in 1961 at the approximate age of ninety. She was buried beside Arthur in Guelph's Woodlawn Cemetery.

Lionel Cutten (Brother)

Lionel and his business partner continued to operate Cutten and Foster Ltd of Toronto, importer of automobile accessories and drapery manufacturers. He and his wife Annie Rowena Adams had one child, a son. Lionel died of a heart attack at his residence in 1938. He was interred at the Mount Pleasant Cemetery in Toronto, where a unique monument by sculptor Emanuel Hahn marks the site.

Constance Cutten Foster (Sister)

Connie was a nurse and lived with her sister Lenore and brother Harry for many years before marrying relatively late in life. She was forty-seven when she wedded George Foster, who managed Cutten Fields for a time. Connie died in 1944, and, like others in her immediate family, the cause of death was coronary thrombosis. She was buried in Woodlawn Cemetery.

Lenore Cutten (Sister)

Lenore remained single and lived at the family home in Guelph. She died in 1945, also from a heart attack. Buried in Woodlawn Cemetery.

Ralph Cutten (Brother)

Ralph operated a successful mortgage brokerage firm with his cousin Edward Chudleigh. He married Ethel Luckham, and they had three children. The family lived in an upscale enclave in Toronto and summered at Windemere in Muskoka. Ralph's fatal heart attack came in 1946.

Harry Cutten (Brother)

A life-long bachelor, Harry lived with his two sisters and spent a great deal of time at Sunny Acres. He died in 1949. Buried in Woodlawn Cemetery.

Joseph Shirley (Nephew)

In 1930, Cutten transferred one of two seats he owned on the Chicago Stock Exchange to his nephew Joseph Shirley. It was a generous gift. At the time, a seat was worth between $35,000 and $50,000.[3] To celebrate the event and introduce his protégé, Cutten made one of his rare public appearances. On 24 May, he walked out on the exchange floor and, with dramatic flair, placed an order with Joseph to buy shares of Majestic Household, thus launching the young man's career.[4] Later that year, the Cuttens attended Joseph's marriage to Luella Barnes in Cincinnati, Ohio.

After a few years as a floor trader at the Chicago Stock Exchange, Arthur Cutten's nephew moved to Cincinnati, where he worked for Procter and Gamble Co. He later established his own business brokering oils and fats. He died in 1986.[5]

Charlie Dunbar

Charles Lawrence Dunbar grew up with Buzz Cutten, attended the same schools and church, and later acted as the speculator's legal counsel in Guelph. His son Angus joined his law practice in 1920, and Charlie remained active in the firm until his death in 1950.[6]

Charles "Chick" Evans

After becoming the first amateur to win both the US Open and US Amateur in 1916, Chick went on to take the Amateur title again in 1920 and was runner-up three times. He was selected to the Walker Cup team in 1922, 1924, and 1928.

He started a scholarship fund that, since its inception, has helped over ten thousand caddies attend colleges and universities across the country. Evans died in 1979 at age eighty-nine.

Charles Mitchell

After his testimony before the Senate Committee on Banking and Currency in 1933, Mitchell resigned in disgrace from National City Bank. He was later indicted for tax evasion. While acquitted of the criminal charges, he lost in a civil procedure and had to pay a $1.1 million settlement to government.

But "Sunshine Charley," the born salesman, was irrepressible. He started up his own financial consulting firm and was named chairman of Blyth & Co., which, under his leadership, became one of the top investment banks. Mitchell died in 1955, his reputation and his fortune restored.[7]

Albert Wiggin

One of the most respected and powerful financiers of his era, Wiggin built Chase National into the largest commercial bank in the world at the time. But he was also lining his pockets by having his family-owned companies participate in pools run by the bank's securities affiliate and by secretly shorting the bank's stock during the Crash.

Ferdinand Pecora said of him, "It is doubtful if there was another instance of a corporate executive who so thoroughly and successfully used his official and fiduciary position for private profit."[8] His abuses exposed, Wiggin retreated from active business life and spent his days quietly adding to his fabulous collection of prints, watercolours, drawings, and books, which passed to the Boston Public Library upon his death in 1951.

Harry Sinclair

Harry Ford Sinclair had been embroiled in scandal long before his association with Cutten. His oil company was one of the firms charged with bribing the US secretary of the interior to obtain a lease on Navy petroleum reserve fields known as Teapot Dome. The Supreme Court ruled that the oil leases had been corruptly obtained, and it invalidated the agreements in 1927. While Harry was acquitted of criminal conspiracy to defraud, he was convicted of contempt of court and served a six-month sentence in a Washington, DC, jail in 1929.

After the takeover of Prairie Oil & Gas and Prairie Pipe Line Company in 1932, thanks in part to Cutten's machinations, Sinclair controlled the eighth largest integrated oil company in America. Harry retired as president in 1949 and died a wealthy man in 1956.

Today there is little evidence that Arthur Cutten passed this way. His spectacular rise to fame, his killings on LaSalle and Wall Streets, and his unparalleled power over the markets are now largely forgotten, obscured by time. Perhaps he bequeathed little to history because he wanted to remain a ghost. Or perhaps later generations, coming through terrible depression and war, chose not to remember.

But if you look hard enough, there are still a few fragments that can be found, traces here and there, of his meteoric life. You may catch a glimpse of the great speculator in a forest clearing, the stony stare of two maidens who inhabit the Chicago Loop, a green fairway that rises above a river, tolling church bells, or a quiet place of death.

Sunny Acres

Cutten's beloved farm, Sunny Acres, was sold in 1937, with the proceeds going to his widow Maud. William "Big Bill" Johnson purchased the property for $145,000, handing over a thick bundle of cash wrapped in paper as payment.[9]

Johnson made his fortune operating a string of gambling halls in Chicago, and it was said that Sunny Acres may have provided some of the beef, pork, and poultry to the kitchens of his various clubs.[10] Ironically, he too was indicted for tax evasion, but in his case a conviction resulted in prison time. He entered Terre Haute federal penitentiary in 1946 and served thirty-two months before being paroled. President Harry Truman granted him a Christmas Eve pardon in 1952, restoring citizenship rights to the convicted felon.

Johnson spent the rest of his life at the old Cutten farm, dying in 1962. In November 1977, the Forest Preserve District of DuPage

*William "Big Bill" Johnson bought Sunny Acres in 1937. Here he is at the Chicago
federal court where he was on trial for income tax evasion.*

County initiated proceedings to gain control of the property and prevent future development. The court granted ownership to the district
and awarded Johnson's heirs $7.3 million in 1978.

The beautiful residence and all the farm buildings were demol-
ished, and the land became part of the Hidden Lake Forest Preserve.

*Statues rescued by Cutten from the old Chicago Board of Trade,
today standing in the LaSalle Street plaza.*

Hiking east of the lake, you may come across a level clearing where the house once stood. That is all there is left of Cutten's magnificent country estate.

Stone Maidens

Another reminder of the Cutten era are the two twelve-foot statues that he had rescued from the old Chicago Board of Trade and brought to his farm. The district discovered them buried in dirt and overgrown with vegetation, and moved them to stand near the entrance to the Danada Forest Preserve in Wheaton. In 2005, the sculptures were returned to the CBOT, and today they stand in a plaza outside its building.

Cutten Fields

After Cutten's death, rumours abounded that he had hidden a big portion of his wealth at his golf club in Guelph. US internal revenue agents reportedly showed up at Cutten Fields searching for stock certificates, bonds, and cash. They tapped walls for secret panels and looked under the rugs and curtains in the clubhouse, so the stories say, and even dug holes in the golf course. Nothing was ever found.[11]

Cutten's estate retained ownership of the golf course, and his family members operated the club at a loss for several years. Finally, in 1939, it was sold for $22,500. Stanley Thompson, who helped design the course, and Donald Ross, a stockbroker in Toronto and owner of the Toronto Maple Leaf Baseball Club, purchased the property.

Ownership passed to six local companies in the 1950s, and Cutten Fields became a private club. Then over the next two decades the University of Guelph (formerly the Ontario Agricultural College) bought up the shares, and it remains the sole owner today.

If you stand on the clubhouse patio, looking down the hill towards the river and the city centre beyond, you may well image Cutten striding through these fields on a rainy day in April 1929. He had recently purchased the Macdonald farm, and he had come to inspect the site. He tarried for a moment, lost in memories of tobogganing here as a boy. You can almost hear him musing that he "wouldn't be surprised" if he came home to stay someday.

Tranquille

The house that Cutten purchased in Guelph, at 13 Stuart Street, remained in the family until 1962. It was then used as a nursing home for a number of years before being restored to a single-family dwelling. Tranquille was designated a cultural heritage property in November 2017.

Portraits

There are three known portraits of Arthur Cutten. One (currently held by Guelph Museums) was painted by Carol Aus in 1925 and shows Cutten wearing a green suit and seated in a chair. In a second smaller portrait, also by Aus, the speculator strikes an almost identical pose but wears a brown suit (this painting hung in the clubhouse at Cutten Fields). The third portrait, painted by Frank O. Salisbury in 1929, shows Cutten again seated, but with a newspaper in his lap. It is documented in Salisbury's papers, which are archived at the National Portrait Gallery in London, England.

The Bells of St George

The twenty-three bells donated by Cutten (along with some new bells added later) still chime every Sunday morning at St George's Anglican Church on Woolwich Street in Guelph. They rang in the new millennium, tolled for those who died on 9/11, and have heralded the joy of Christmas for some one hundred years.[12]

Cemetery Monument

The towering obelisk at Woodlawn Cemetery in Guelph still stands solitary watch over the Cutten family members buried there.

CHAPTER SIXTEEN

The Measure of a Man

Arthur Cutten gained tremendous fortune and fame through his audacious exploits in the grain and stock markets of the 1920s. He was the shining example of the self-made man, the hero who struggled against the odds to emerge victorious in his quest. Celebrated by his generation, he was the prototypical outsider, a popular rogue of sorts, challenging the establishment, taking enormous risks, doing things his way and winning. There was something glamourous and admirable in this.

Born into an upper-middle-class family, Buzz could have remained in Guelph, comfortable and content. But, early on, he felt the tug of adventure, and he wanted to make his way in the world. And then when his father's banking business failed and his shameful financial dealings were revealed, the young man had all the more reason to leave his hometown. He was determined to pursue a path that would take him all the way to the top, sure that with enough money and influence, he could wipe clean the stain on the family name.

Arthur learned the hard lessons of the markets over a period of fifteen years. It was an arduous apprenticeship, and his masters were of the old school, instilling in him the virtues of individualism, self-reliance, hard work, and steely resolve.

"Sometimes I feel as if there really were giants in those days," Cutten reminisced.[1] He absorbed their teachings, and he became like them. There was no room for pity, no quarter given to those who failed. It was a tough world, and only tough men survived.

That he was skilful and bold, there is no question. None had ever swung as big a line in the pits or traded such a volume on the stock exchange as Arthur Cutten. He reached beyond what anyone else had ever dared. "I have traded more heavily than any other individual who ever stood in the wheat pit," he rightly asserted. "I have had big adventures in Wall Street."[2]

He succeeded. Spectacularly. He made a killing. By the standards of his time, he was a winner, a conqueror. He had achieved what he set out to do. He was the "Wheat King," he was "Bull Cutten," the famous speculator who ruled the markets in the heady days of the Roaring Twenties.

But then times changed. With the sickening Crash of '29 and the long economic malaise that followed, public attitudes turned against the tycoons and barons of finance. They were no longer held in awe; rather, they came to be scorned and reviled for the way they had gamed the system, for rigging the markets in their favour and suckering the little guys with promises of easy money.

In the dark era of the Great Depression, with war looming on the horizon, there was little sympathy for men such as Cutten. He went from icon to infamy as the public learned how he had amassed his fortune. He was blamed for the destruction of farm incomes, the loss of life savings, and the hardship and ruin that engulfed America.

He became a pariah, despised for his cold calculations that earned him millions and left a trail of human wreckage behind.

And then he sank from view. Like the statues in his garden, his story was forgotten, buried, and obliterated in the dust of time.

Hero or villain?

By the scorecard of his day, he was the undisputed champion. He made a mountain of money. He bested his enemies. He had one of the most sensational runs in the history of the markets.

Those who judge him today will, no doubt, find him a flawed and morally bankrupt character. A dissembler. A swindler.

In the final analysis, he is probably all these things.

Arthur Cutten was the perfect product of his age. As he had in his youth, he played for all the marbles and he played for keeps. He was the ultimate opportunist, and he was better at it than anyone else. With sleight of hand, he transmuted stocks and grains into gold. And for a time, everyone believed.

Cutten's Way

Arthur Cutten spent years honing his skills and perfecting his techniques in the grain pits of Chicago and stock exchange of New York. What were the key lessons he learned? Unlike Jesse Livermore, he did not leave a "how to" manual or guidebook to his trading secrets. But in interviews and various media articles, he did reveal at least the basic principles he followed in his remarkable rise to riches. Herewith, the core tenets of Cutten's Way.[1]

At heart, he was a gambler. He loved the thrill of the game. Winning was important because money conferred status. But the true joy came from being "right."

> It has been my experience that everybody likes to make money. And now that we understand each other, I can confess to another satisfaction which is by way of being an extra dividend on any successful trading operation. This is the chance one gets to say, "I told you so." And that, I have discovered, is something else common to all mankind.

He speculated intelligently. Cutten did his homework.

> I did not have a single advantage over others who traded except as these advantages existed within my own skull.
> A man can't expect to make money on a stock if he buys without the faintest notion of what the stock is – as so many fools do.[2]

He trusted his own wits and shunned market gossip, tips, and advice.

> I soon realized that the loudest voice was not necessarily the biggest trader.
> I have had little faith in the judgement of other people.
> Don't gamble on what the other fellow says.[3]

For Cutten, nerve and confidence were essential. Once he determined a course of action, he committed fully. There were no half measures.

> Confidence in yourself is something you must have if you are going to be a successful speculator.
> To be able to stick in a risky position without shattering your nerves, you must have a continuing confidence in the judgment that caused you to take that position in the first place. I have had confidence in my own judgment always.
> Each time you trade you are backing your opinion that the other fellow, the one who buys from or sells to you, is wrong.

If he was making money in the market, he let his profits pile up. But when the market turned against him, he would "cut 'n' run."

> The way to make money was to be as quick as possible in taking a loss, but to be slow in taking profits.
> Most of my success has been due to my hanging on while my profits mounted. There is the big secret. Do with it what you will.
> Whenever he [Jim Patten] found himself wrong, he could run out of the market like a scared cat. That was one of the reasons he was successful. He knew he could not make a market go his way by being stubborn.

Cutten accepted his losses.

> There would be no thrill in winning if you never lost.

But ultimately, to survive, he had to take more out of the market than he gave up.

> If he [the speculator] profits three times out of four, he should be satisfied. If he persists in losing three times out of four, he soon loses the means to speculate.

Cutten started by scalping, taking small and frequent positions, but realized that the big money came from catching the big waves.

> Mine was not the in-and-out speculation of so many who lost their reason in the bull market.
> I was constantly striving to sense the broad swings of the market and to understand the reasons for them.

He cautioned against over-diversification.
Advising a friend who held seventeen stocks in his portfolio, he stated:

> You can't hope to watch that many even on the ticker. You'd have extraordinary difficulty in arriving at sound conclusions regarding them. You ought to trim down that list. Never be in more than four or five at a time. Four is plenty. So many stocks are confusing and interfere with your judgment. You can't make money that way.

A bull or a bear, it mattered not to Cutten. A dead-accurate sense of direction and timing, that's what counted.

> As you would say of an athlete, my timing had been good. I had been, as we say in the grain trade, right.

Be prepared for some pain along the way.

> The blows a speculator takes when he loses are hard jolts to his nervous system.
> When you lose, you sweat blood.

In a moment of candour, Cutten acknowledged that most small investors will fail miserably.

> I have taken my bit out of the market – oh quite a bit – but I would advise other men to stay away from it. If I had a son – which I haven't – I would keep him far away. I wouldn't let him touch it with a 10-foot pole. There are so many sorry wrecks down there in the pits.[4]

CHRONOLOGY

1870–90   Born 6 July 1870, in Guelph, Ontario, one of nine children born to Walter Hoyt and Annie (MacFadden) Cutten.

Attends Trinity College School (1883–84) and Guelph Collegiate Institute.

Works as a clerk at the US Consulate in Guelph.

The Guelph Banking Company fails in 1888. His father is ruined financially and disgraced in the community.

1890   Arthur boards a train for Chicago. Holds a series of menial jobs.

1891   Gains employment with A.S. White & Co., a commodity brokerage firm.

1896   On 11 November becomes a member of the Chicago Board of Trade.

1904   Quits A.S. White and begins to trade for himself.

1905   Buys Tranquille, a home for his family in Guelph.

1906   12 May, marries Maud Boomer.

1907   October, a financial crisis and a panic in the markets. Cutten suffers losses in wheat, Jesse Livermore makes $3 million on Wall Street.

1912   Cutten scores in the corn market. Purchases land near
            Downers Grove and begins to build Sunny Acres, his
            rural estate.

1916   On 14 July becomes a naturalized citizen of the
            United States.

1922   27 March, armed robbers raid Sunny Acres and leave
            the Cuttens and staff to die in a locked vault. Arthur
            vows vengeance and initiates eight-year manhunt for
            the culprits.

            Arthur's corner in wheat broken when Board of Trade
            invokes emergency delivery rule.

1924–25 Gains fame as the "Wheat King." Livermore launches
            bear raid when Cutten is away from the markets, but
            Arthur holds firm and emerges $15 million richer. CBOT's
            Business Conduct Committee pressures him to sell part
            of his holdings.

1926–29 Focuses his operations on Wall Street. Over a three-year
            period, his fortune grows to more than $100 million.
            Massive trading for his own accounts and also runs pools
            in league with the Fisher brothers, Billy Durant, George
            Breen, and others.

            April 1929, announcement of $1 million gift to his
            hometown, including a golf course, sports complex,
            hotel, and conference centre.

            17 July 1929, meets with Joseph Kennedy to try to
            convince him to remain fully invested in the market.
            Kennedy ultimately rejects the advice.

            October 1929, the stock market tanks. About half of
            Cutten's paper profits are wiped out. Livermore makes
            millions shorting stocks.

8 November 1929. His wife Maud and her friends are robbed on their way home from the opera. James Riordon, head of the County Trust Bank, dies by suicide.

1930–33   Cutten returns to the grain markets in Chicago, once more trading millions of bushels, most often on the short side.

9 June 1930, his friend Jake Lingle, crime reporter for the *Chicago Tribune*, is gunned down in a mob hit.

15 January 1931, Edson White, one of Arthur's friends from their boarding house days, dies in a fall from his seventh-floor apartment.

9 November 1933, brought before the US Senate Committee on Banking and Currency (Pecora Commission) to testify about his stock market activities, particularly his manipulation of Sinclair Consolidated Oil shares.

1934   9 April, charged under the Grain Futures Act. The government seeks to ban him from the grain pits. Case goes all the way to the US Supreme Court.

1935   November, suffers a heart attack.

1936   March–April, indicted on charges of income tax evasion.

18 May, government loses bid to bar Cutten from grain trading.

24 June, dies at the Edgewater Beach Hotel.

Revealed in probate court that his assets worth only about $350,000.

1940   28 November, Jesse Livermore blows his brains out in a cloakroom at the Sherry-Netherland hotel.

1948   Multi-year search fails to find Cutten's missing
            millions. The probate court finally closes the estate on
            23 December 1948.

1961   His wife Maud dies at the approximate age of ninety.

NOTES

Chapter One

1 *Chicago Tribune*, 29 May 1936, 27.
2 *Detroit Free Press*, 29 May 1936, 23.
3 Cutten with Sparkes, "Story of a Speculator," 3 December 1932.
4 Ibid., 10 December 1932.
5 *Maclean's*, 15 August 1931.
6 *Toronto Star*, 1 September 1934.
7 Jenkins, "Lone Wolf of the Wheat Pit," 18.
8 *Fadedgenes: A Chronicle of the People of the Methodist Church in Canada*, "William Dyson – Wesleyan Methodist Member Norfolk St Guelph Wellington County," 12 October 2012, https://krassoc.wordpress.com/2012/10/12/william-dyson-wesleyan-methodist-member-norfolk-st-guelph-wellington-county/.
9 Cutten with Sparkes, "Story of a Speculator," 19 November 1932.
10 *Toronto Telegram*, 20 February 1929.
11 *Upper Canada Law Journal*, 311.
12 1881 Census of Canada.
13 Most of the information about Cutten's ancestry comes from Cutten, *Genealogy of the Cutten Family of Nova Scotia*.
14 Elliott, *Legislative Assembly of Nova Scotia*, 46, 245.
15 Elgin County Branch of the Ontario Genealogical Society, *County Places of Worship*.
16 1851 Census of Canada West.
17 *Canada Directory for 1857–58*.
18 Goodspeed and Goodspeed, *History of the County of Middlesex*; *McAlpine's London City and County of Middlesex Directory, 1875*; *London City Business Directory, 1876–1877*.
19 *White's London City and Middlesex County Directory, 1881–1882*, 28.
20 Thorning, "Hayseed Capitalists."
21 *Guelph Mercury*, 31 January 1888.
22 *Monetary Times*, 3 February 1888.
23 Cutten with Sparkes, "Story of a Speculator," 19 November 1932.
24 Ibid.

25 Ibid.
26 *New York Times*, 3 February 1888.
27 Thorning, "Hayseed Capitalists."
28 *Guelph Mercury*, 31 January 1888.
29 Ibid., 1 February 1888.
30 Thorning, "Hayseed Capitalists."
31 *Guelph Mercury*, 19 March 1888.
32 Thorning, "Irregular Banking Practices."
33 Ibid.
34 Ibid.
35 Cutten's naturalization documentation, *US Department of Labor, Immigration and Naturalization Services*, Certificate No. P 17382.
36 1861 Census of Canada.
37 Mulvany, *Toronto Past and Present*, 146.
38 Thorning, "Guelph Banking Company," 10.
39 *New York Sun*, 18 June 1887, 2.
40 *Montreal Gazette*, 13 February 1888, 1.
41 Thorning, "Hayseed Capitalists."
42 *Kansas City Age*, 16 September 1892, 6.
43 *Walton Reporter* (Walton, Kansas), 17 March 1893, 2.

Chapter Two

1   Cutten with Sparkes, "Story of a Speculator," 19 November 1932.
2   Ibid.
3   Ibid.
4   *New York Times*, 30 April 1891, 1.
5   Cutten with Sparkes, "Story of a Speculator," 19 November 1932.
6   Dies, *Street of Adventure*.
7   Jenkins, "Lone Wolf of the Wheat Pit."
8   Cutten with Sparkes, "Story of a Speculator," 19 November 1932.
9   Ibid.
10 *Collingwood Bulletin*, 27 October 1899, 1.
11 Jenkins, "Lone Wolf of the Wheat Pit."
12 Baker and Hahn, *Cotton Kings*.
13 Cutten with Sparkes, "Story of a Speculator," 19 November 1932.
14 Fetherling, *Gold Diggers*.
15 Chase, *Delta Upsilon Quinquennial Catalogue*.
16 *Evanston Directory*, Evanston Press Company, 1893–96.
17 US Passport Application, 1922, roll 1831, certificate 118124.

18 Smitten, *Jesse Livermore*, 77.
19 US Federal Census, 1900; Taylor, *History of the Board of Trade*, 3:335; *Chicago Tribune*, 25 October 1918, 11.
20 Jenkins, "Lone Wolf of the Wheat Pit."
21 US Passport Application, certificate 74461, 8 April 1919.
22 Canadian County Atlas Digital Project, http://digital.library.mcgill.ca/countyatlas/default.htm.
23 Cobban, *Cities of Oil*, 29.
24 *Montreal Gazette*, 28 May 1880, 1.
25 *OAC (Ontario Agricultural College) Review* 42, no. 7 (March 1930): 396–7.
26 Forbes, *Men Who Are Making America*, 414–19.
27 1900 US Federal Census.
28 1920 US Federal Census.
29 Jenkins, "Lone Wolf of the Wheat Pit."
30 *New York Times*, 3 January 1923, 1.
31 *Boys' Life: The Boy Scouts' Magazine*, March 1923, 27.
32 Cutten with Sparkes, "Story of a Speculator," 19 November 1932.
33 *Daily Sun-Times* (Owen Sound, ON), 6 January 1923, 6.
34 *Time*, 29 August 1927.
35 *New York Times*, 16 January 1931.
36 Ibid.
37 *Chicago Tribune*, 16 January 1931, 1.
38 *Time*, 26 January 1931.

Chapter Three

1 Cutten with Sparkes, "Story of a Speculator," 3 December 1932.
2 Ibid., 19 November 1932.
3 Smitten, *Jesse Livermore*, 59.
4 *Chicago Tribune*, 9 December 1928, 3.
5 Cutten with Sparkes, "Story of a Speculator," 26 November 1932.
6 Ibid.
7 Patten with Sparkes, "'In the Wheat Pit," 3 September 1927.
8 Baker and Hahn, *Cotton Kings*.
9 Greising and Morse, *Brokers, Bagmen, and Moles*, 53–4.
10 *Morning Oregonian*, 12 March 1910.
11 Patten with Sparkes, "In the Wheat Pit," 1 October 1927.
12 Ibid.; Cutten with Sparkes, "Story of a Speculator," 3 December 1932.
13 *Chicago Tribune*, 9 December 1928, 3.
14 Patten with Sparkes, "In the Wheat Pit," 17 September 1927.

Chapter Four

1 Robert McCarter, *Frank Lloyd Wright*; Frank Lloyd Wright Foundation Archives.
2 Hahin, "Hidden History of Hidden Lake"; *Chicago Tribune*, 16 February 1978, B1.
3 Thompson, *Around the Arboretum.*
4 *Chicago Tribune*, 16 July 1924, 3.
5 Much of the information about Sunny Acres was provided by James Nelson Jr, son of the farm manager. James Jr was born and raised on the farm, and graciously agreed to be interviewed when in his ninety-first year.
6 Cutten with Sparkes, "Story of a Speculator," 26 November 1932.
7 Thompson, *Around the Arboretum.*
8 Cutten with Sparkes, "Story of a Speculator," 10 December 1932.
9 1910 and 1920 US Federal Census.
10 From correspondence with Ted Shirley, grandson of Joseph Shirley.
11 *Chicago Tribune*, 9 May 1930, 30.
12 Cooke, "History of Woodlawn Cemetery."
13 *Mail and Empire*, 13 April 1929.
14 *New York Times*, 10 August 1921, 21.
15 *Hutchinson News* (Hutchinson, Kansas), 26 January 1917, 11.
16 Probate Court of Cook County, Illinois, *In The Matter of the Estate of Arthur W. Cutten, Deceased*, docket 356, p. 335, file 36P-5440.
17 *Chicago Tribune*, 24 March 1920, 15.
18 Ibid., 10 March 1922.
19 *American Elevator and Grain Trade*, 642, https://archive.org/details/CAT31053470336.
20 Information about Mitchell from Lenora H. King, editor and publisher, *Southwest Blue Book 1923–1924*, October 1923; information about Reynolds from *Chicago Tribune*, 5 September 1933, 22.

Chapter Five

1 Cutten with Sparkes, "Story of a Speculator," 26 November 1932.
2 Most of the information about the robbery at Sunny Acres is from press reports as well as from Savage, "Private Vengeance of Arthur Cutten," which is the most complete and accurate account.
3 Cutten with Sparkes, "Story of a Speculator," 10 December 1932.
4 *Chicago Tribune*, 9 April 1931, 6.
5 Associated Press, 25 November 1932.

Chapter Six

1 Cutten with Sparkes, "Story of a Speculator," 26 November 1932.
2 Ibid.
3 Ibid., 10 December 1932.
4 *Chicago Tribune*, 15 July 1924, 1.
5 *Time*, 25 May 1925.
6 *New York Times*, 6 September 1925, 3.
7 Cutten with Sparkes, "Story of a Speculator," 26 November 1932.
8 *Toronto Telegram*, 20 February 1929.
9 *Chicago Tribune*, 10 October 1925.
10 Cutten with Sparkes, "Story of a Speculator," 3 December 1932.
11 *Chicago Tribune*, 20 March 1926, 1.
12 Brett, *Cutten Club 50th Anniversary Book*, 15.

Chapter Seven

1 Cutten with Sparkes, "Story of a Speculator," 10 December 1932.
2 *New York Times*, 15 November 1927.
3 "Stock Exchange Practices," *Report of the Senate Committee on Banking and Currency*, 44.
4 *Chicago Central Business and Office Building Directory 1928* (Winters Publishing Company). Also *Polk's Directory*, 1928–29.
5 *Daily Northwestern*, Student newspaper of Northwestern University, 25 June 1929; "Guelph's Fairy Godfather," *Canadian Golfer* 14, no. 12 (1929): 949–50.
6 *Chicago Tribune*, 11 March 1936, 1.
7 *Business Week*, 18 November 1931, 24.
8 Cutten with Sparkes, "Story of a Speculator," 3 December 1932.
9 *Time*, 10 December 1932.
10 US Senate, *Hearings on Stock Exchange Practices before the Committee on Banking and Currency*, 72d Congress, pursuant to S. Res. 84, pt. 2, 681–5.
11 Securities and Exchange Commission, *Report on Abuses and Deficiencies*.
12 Ibid., 270.
13 US Senate, *Hearings on Stock Exchange Practices before the Committee on Banking and Currency*, 72d Congress.
14 Sparling, *Mystery Men of Wall Street*.
15 James Feron, "Country Clubs Sell a New Image," *New York Times*, 22 July 1979.
16 Parker, *Unmasking Wall Street*, 112.
17 *Chicago Daily Tribune*, 21 April 1928.

18 Ibid., 28 September 1928.
19 *New York Times*, 30 September 1928.
20 *Chicago Daily Tribune*, 17 November 1928.
21 *New York Times*, 20 April 1928, 25.
22 *Chicagoan* 6, no. 3 (November 1928): 36.
23 *Chicago Tribune*, 26 February 1935, 17.
24 *Time*, 10 December 1928.
25 *Courier-News* (Bridgewater, New Jersey), 11 December 1928, 11.
26 Cutten with Sparkes, "Story of a Speculator," 19 November 1932.
27 Description of Livermore's office from Smitten, *Jesse Livermore*.
28 *Detroit Free Press*, 4 November 1928.
29 Cutten with Sparkes, "Story of a Speculator," 3 December 1932.
30 Automotive Hall of Fame, https://www.automotivehalloffame.org/honoree/charles-t-fisher/.
31 Coachbuilt.com, http://www.coachbuilt.com/bui/f/fisher/fisher.htm.
32 Automotive Hall of Fame.
33 Jacobus, *Fisher Body Craftsman's Guild*, 23.
34 Alef, *Fabulous Fisher Brothers*.
35 Ingham, *Biographical Dictionary of American Business Leaders*, 1:387.
36 Fisher, *100 Minds That Made the Market*.
37 *Baltimore Evening Sun*, 6 March 1972, C12.
38 Clayton, *Clayton's Quaker Cook Book*, 92, https://www.gutenberg.org/files/38823/38823-h/38823-h.htm#Page_92. See also *Pacific Unitarian*, vol. 32, January 1923, San Francisco, 99–100, https://archive.org/stream/pacificunitari321923wilb/pacificunitari321923wilb_djvu.txt.
39 *Philadelphia Inquirer*, 11 March 1917, 63.
40 *Ancestry.com*, New York, US Extracted Marriage Index, 1866–1937.
41 *San Francisco Recorder*, 18 July 1925, 9.
42 *Baltimore Evening Sun*, 6 March 1972, C12.
43 *Philadelphia Inquirer*, 22 October 1944, 3.
44 *Fort Worth Star-Telegram*, 9 February 1937, 1.
45 *Los Angeles Times*, 24 June 1951, 1.
46 Fisher, "William C. 'Billy' Durant."
47 Niemeyer and Flink, *General of General Motors*.
48 Durant, *My Father*.
49 See "Durant, William Craypo," Encyclopedia.com, last updated 27 June 2018, https://www.encyclopedia.com/people/social-sciences-and-law/business-leaders/william-crapo-durant.
50 Pound, *Turning Wheel*, 120–1.
51 Durant, *My Father*.

52 Gustin, *Billy Durant*.
53 Pound, *Turning Wheel*.
54 Gustin, *Billy Durant*.
55 Ibid.
56 Niemeyer and Flink, *General of General Motors*.
57 Chrysler with Sparkes, *Life of an American Workman*.
58 Fisher, *100 Minds That Made the Market*.
59 Fisher, "William C. 'Billy' Durant."
60 Niemeyer and Flink, *General of General Motors*; Folsom, "Billy Durant."
61 Gustin, *Billy Durant*.
62 Fisher, "'William C. 'Billy' Durant."
63 1900 US Federal Census.
64 1940 US Federal Census.
65 *New York Daily News*, Obituary, 3 January 1948, 115.
66 World War I Selective Service System Draft Registration Cards, 1917–1918. Registration State: New York; Registration County: Queens; Roll: 1787092; Draft Board: 174.
67 Thomas and Morgan-Witts, *Day the Bubble Burst*.
68 Meehan, writing about his grandparents, in Meehan, *My American Story*.
69 1930 US Federal Census.
70 Petition for Naturalization, no. 21355, 1919, US Department of Labour.
71 *New York Daily News*, Obituary, 3 January 1948, 115.
72 Geisst, *Wall Street*, 184.
73 Blumenthal, *Six Days in October*.
74 Thomas and Morgan-Witts, *Day the Bubble Burst*.
75 Ibid.
76 Nations, *History of the United States in Five Crashes*.
77 *Time*, 7 December 1936.
78 Thomas and Morgan-Witts, *Day the Bubble Burst*.
79 Markham, *Financial History of the United States*, 2:143.
80 1870 US Federal Census.
81 *New York Times*, 3 July 1957, 23.
82 Sparling, *Mystery Men of Wall Street*, 228.
83 *New York Times*, 30 October 1916, 9.
84 *Dayton Daily News* (Ohio), 10 September 1916, 22.
85 US Senate, *Stock Exchange Practices, Hearings before the Committee on Banking and Currency*, 72d Congress.
86 *Motorboating: The Yachtsmen's Magazine*, 47, no. 4 (April 1931), 40–1.
87 *Ithaca Journal* (New York), 26 January 1949, 15.

Chapter Eight

1 *Toronto Star*, 11 April 1929.
2 Ibid., 13 April 1929.
3 Ibid.
4 *Mail and Empire*, 2 April 1929.
5 "The Cutten Papers," *Weekend Magazine*, 20 October 1979.
6 *Mail and Empire*, 12 April 1929; *Toronto Star*, 13 April 1929.
7 Brett, *Cutten Club 50th Anniversary Book*.
8 Ibid.
9 Probate Court of Cook County, Illinois, *In The Matter of the Estate of Arthur W. Cutten, Deceased*, docket 356, p. 335, file 36P-5440, Report of Administrator with Respect to Discovery of Items Scheduled in Second Supplemental Inventory, 7 August 1937.

Chapter Nine

1 Crowther, "Everybody Ought to Be Rich."
2 *Democrat and Chronicle* (Rochester, NY), 17 August 1929.
3 *Wall Street Journal*, 1 October 1929.
4 *New York Times*, 15 October 1929.
5 Thomas and Morgan-Witts, *Day the Bubble Burst*.
6 *New York Times*, 20 October 1929.
7 Ibid., 22 October 1929.
8 Farber, *Everybody Ought to Be Rich*, 32.
9 Reynolds, "History and Significance of John Jakob Raskob."
10 Maynard, "Archmere."
11 Farber, *Everybody Ought to Be Rich*, 172.
12 Ibid., 273–4.
13 *Chicago Tribune*, 28 September 1928, 3.
14 Farber, *Everybody Ought to Be Rich*, 242.
15 Ibid., 253.
16 Reynolds, "History and Significance of John Jakob Raskob."
17 "Rethinking Raskob," *Forbes*, posted 9 October 2000, https://www.forbes.com/forbes/2000/1009/6610064a.html#351018c33c00.
18 Aerospaceweb.org, "B-25 Empire State Building Collision," http://www.aerospaceweb.org/question/history/q0311.shtml.
19 Hagely Museum and Library, Manuscripts and Archives Department, "Facts about the American Liberty League," John J. Raskob Papers (Accession 0473), https://digital.hagley.org/m473_20100816_014#page/1/mode/2up.

20 Hagley Museum and Library, Manuscripts and Archives Department, John J. Raskob Papers, biographical note, https://findingaids.hagley.org/repositories/3/resources/847.

21 Colby, *Du Pont Dynasty*.

22 *New York Times*, 1 December 1938, 25.

Chapter Ten

1 *New York Times*, 12 August 1928, 2.

2 US Senate, *Stock Exchange Practices, Report of the Committee on Banking and Currency*, pursuant to S. Res. 84 (72d Congress) and S. Res. 56 and S. Res. 97 (73d Congress), 1934.

3 Ibid.

4 Galbraith, *Great Crash*.

5 Blumenthal, *Six Days in October*, 38.

6 Lough, *No More Champagne*.

7 Associated Press, 25 October 1929.

8 *Toronto Star*, 25 October 1929.

9 *Globe*, 26 October 1929.

10 *Chicago Tribune*, 29 October 1929, 31.

11 "The Cutten Papers," *Weekend Magazine*, 20 October 1979.

12 Cutten with Sparkes, "Story of a Speculator," 3 December 1932.

13 *Des Moines Tribune*, 3 November 1931, 4; *New York World*, 30 October 1929. See also Fisher, *100 Minds That Made the Market*.

Chapter Eleven

1 Account of robbery from *Chicago Tribune*, 9 November 1929, 1; and *Sterling Daily Gazette* (Sterling, Illinois), 9 November 1929, 1.

2 Cutten with Sparkes, "Story of a Speculator," 10 December 1932.

3 Associated Press in the *Sheboygan Press* (Wisconsin), 22 March 1934, 1; International News Service (INS) in the *St Louis Star and Times*, 22 March 1934, 4.

Chapter Twelve

1 Cutten with Sparkes, "Story of a Speculator," 10 December 1932.

2 Ferris, *Grain Traders*, 191.

3 *Toronto Star*, 14 May 1934.

4 Ferris, *Grain Traders*, 192–3.

5 Cutten's trading activities during this period are sourced from National Archives, *Secretary of Agriculture v. Arthur Cutten*.

6 *Baltimore Sun*, 13 April 1934, 4.
7 *New York Times*, 24 July 1932, F4.
8 United Press, 5 August 1932.
9 *Wisconsin State Journal* (Madison, Wisconsin), 27 January 1931, 18.
10 Cutten with Sparkes, "Story of a Speculator," 10 December 1932.
11 Boettiger, "Solution of the Lingle Murder."
12 Fred Pasley, *Al Capone*, 290.
13 United Press, 10 June 1930.
14 *Chicago Tribune*, 10 June 1930, 1.
15 Cutten with Sparkes, "Story of a Speculator," 10 December 1932.
16 1930 US Federal Census.
17 Boettiger, "Solution of the Lingle Murder."
18 Pasley, *Al Capone*, 274.
19 Boettiger, "Solution of the Lingle Murder."
20 *Chicago Tribune*, 12 June 1930, 1.
21 Ibid., 10 June 1930, 1.
22 Krajicek, "Corrupt Chicago Tribune Newsman."
23 Ibid.
24 *Chicago Tribune*, 1 July 1930, 2.

Chapter Thirteen

1 Excerpts from US Senate, *Hearings on Stock Exchange Practices before the Committee on Banking and Currency*, 73d Congress, pursuant to S. Res. 84 and S. Res. 56, pt. 6, 3055–120.
2 Brinkley, "When Washington Took On Wall Street."
3 Pecora, *Wall Street under Oath*.
4 Brinkley, "When Washington Took On Wall Street"; King, "Man Who Busted the Banksters."
5 *Time*, 2 June 1933.
6 Perino, *Hellhound of Wall Street*.
7 Ibid.
8 King, "Man Who Busted the Banksters."
9 Perino, *Hellhound of Wall Street*.
10 Chernow, *House of Morgan*; John Brooks, "Millionaire and the Midget."
11 Fisher, *100 Minds That Made the Market*.
12 Perino, *Hellhound of Wall Street*.

Chapter Fourteen

1 *Decatur Daily Review*, 12 April 1934, 17.
2 *Congressional Record*, 73d Cong., 2d sess., 1934, 78, pt. 10: 10446.

3 Ibid.

4 *Chicago Tribune*, 15 May 1934, 27.

5 Ibid., 12 May 1934, 31.

6 *St Louis Post-Dispatch*, 12 January 1935.

7 *Chicago Tribune*, 27 December 1935, 4.

8 US Supreme Court, *Wallace v. Cutten*, 298 US 229 (1936), no. 747.

9 *Chicago Tribune*, 29 May 1936, 27.

10 *Windsor Star*, 24 June 1936, 1.

11 *Chicago Tribune*, 25 June 1936, 25.

12 Ibid., 26 June 1936, 32.

13 Ibid., 23 July 1936, 5. Maud Cutten renounced her right to become executrix of the estate and asked the probate court to appoint instead the American National Bank & Trust Company as administrator.

14 *Chicago Tribune*, 26 July 1936, 5.

15 Ibid., 4 June 1937, 20

16 Probate Court of Cook County, Illinois, *In the Matter of the Estate of Arthur W. Cutten, Deceased*, docket 356, p. 335, file 36P-5440, Report of Administrator with Respect to Discovery of Items Scheduled in Second Supplemental Inventory, 7 August 1937.

17 Memos from K.F. Hannan, Director of Estates Investigation Branch, to C.S. Walters, Deputy Provincial Treasurer, Estates Investigations, Treasury nos. 16D and 16J, RG 6-15, B290537, Archives of Ontario.

18 *Jackson v. Jackson et al.*, Circuit Court of Cook County, docket B156351, Second Amended and Supplemental Complaint of Florence May Jackson, 13 February 1936.

19 *Globe and Mail*, 7 September 1937.

20 US Senate, *Hearings on Stock Exchange Practices before the Committee on Banking and Currency*, 73d Congress, pursuant to S. Res. 84 and S. Res. 56, pt. 6, 3055–120.

21 Cutten with Sparkes, "Story of a Speculator," 3 December 1932.

22 *Chicago Tribune*, 24 December 1948, 22.

Chapter Fifteen

1 *Brooklyn Daily Eagle*, 29 November 1940, 7.

2 Smitten, *Jesse Livermore*, 278–82.

3 *Albuquerque Journal*, 11 May 1930, 8; *Chicago Tribune*, 9 May 1930, 30.

4 *Chicago Tribune*, 25 May 1930, 37.

5 *Cincinnati Enquirer*, 23 December 1986, 13.

6 *Guelph Mercury*, 3 March 1950.

7 Huertas and Silverman, "Charles E. Mitchell," 81–103.

8 Pecora, *Wall Street under Oath*.

9 *Chicago Tribune*, 9 May 1937, 26; *Chicago Tribune*, 31 August 1940, 11.

10 Hahin, "Hidden History of Hidden Lake," 3.

11 Brett, *Cutten Club 50th Anniversary Book.*

12 "The Bells of St. George," *Niagara Anglican*, May 2006, 5.

Chapter Sixteen

1 Cutten with Sparkes, "Story of a Speculator," 19 November 1932.

2 Ibid.

Appendix

1 All quotes, unless noted below, are from Cutten's memoirs, "The Story of a Speculator," which he wrote with Boyden Sparkes, published by the *Saturday Evening Post*, 19 November, 26 November, 3 December, and 10 December 1932.

2 Dies, *Street of Adventure*, 33.

3 *Toronto World*, 28 September 1924.

4 *Chicago Tribune*, 16 July 1924, 3.

BIBLIOGRAPHY

Newspapers, Magazines, and Journals

Albuquerque Journal
American Elevator and Grain Trade
Baltimore Sun
Boy's Life, The Boy Scouts' Magazine
Business Week
Business History Review
Canadian Golfer
Chicago Tribune
Chicagoan
Cincinnati Enquirer
Collingwood Bulletin (Collingwood, Ontario)
Courier-News (Bridgewater, New Jersey)
Daily Northwestern (Northwestern University student newspaper)
Dayton Daily News
Decatur Daily Review
Democrat and Chronicle (Rochester, New York)
Des Moines Tribune
Detroit Free Press
Fort Worth Star-Telegram
Globe (Toronto)
Globe and Mail
Guelph Mercury
Harper's Weekly
Hutchinson News (Hutchinson, Kansas)
Ithaca Journal (Ithaca, New York),
Kansas City Age
Kansas City Star
Ladies' Home Journal
Los Angeles Times
Maclean's
Mail and Empire (Toronto)
Monetary Times
Montreal Gazette
Morning Oregonian (Portland, Oregon)
Motorboating: The Yachtsmen's Magazine
New York Sun
New York Times
New York World
OAC (Ontario Agricultural College) Review
Philadelphia Inquirer
Real Detective Tales and Mystery Stories
Sheboygan Press (Sheboygan, Wisconsin)
St Louis Post-Dispatch
St Louis Star and Times
Sterling Daily Gazette (Sterling, Illinois)
Sun-Times (Owen Sound, Ontario)
Time
Toronto Star
Toronto Telegram
Toronto World
Wall Street Journal
Walton Reporter (Walton, Kansas)
Weekend Magazine
Western Architect
Windsor Star (Windsor, Ontario)
Wisconsin State Journal (Madison, Wisconsin)

Archives

Archives of Ontario, RG 6-15, B290537, Treasury No. 16D and 16J, Estates Investigations, memos from K.F. Hannan, Director of Estates Investigation Branch, to C.S. Walters, Deputy Provincial Treasurer

Chicago History Museum

Circuit Court of Cook County, *Jackson v. Jackson et al.*, docket B156351

Frank Lloyd Wright Foundation Archives: architectural drawings, ca. 1885–1959, Avery Architectural & Fine Arts Library, Columbia University, New York

Guelph Public Library

Guelph Museums

General Motors Heritage Center

Hagley Museum and Library

Library of Congress, Prints and Photographs Division

National Archives, *Secretary of Agriculture v. Arthur Cutten*, Grain Futures Administration, docket 7, Record Group 180

Probate Court of Cook County, docket 356, p. 335, file 36P-5440, *Report of Administrator with Respect to Discovery of Items Scheduled in Second Supplemental Inventory*, 7 August 1937

Securities and Exchange Commission. *A Report on Abuses and Deficiencies in the Organization and Operation of Investment Trusts and Investment Companies*, pt. 3, chap. 2. Washington: US Government Printing Office, 1940

US Senate. *Hearings on Stock Exchange Practices before the Committee on Banking and Currency.* 72d Congress, Pursuant to S. Res. 84, pt. 2, 681–5

– *Stock Exchange Practices, Report of the Committee on Banking and Currency.* Pursuant to S. Res. 84 (72d Congress) and S. Res. 56 and S. Res. 97 (73d Congress), 1934

– *Stock Exchange Practices, Hearings before the Committee on Banking and Currency*, 72d Congress, Pursuant to S. Res. 84, pt. 2.

Upper Canada Law Journal, n.s., vol. 3. Toronto: W.C. Chewett & Co., 1867

Other Sources

Alef, Daniel. *The Fabulous Fisher Brothers: The Rothschilds of America.* Santa Barbara: Titans of Fortune Publishing, first Kindle edition, 2009.

Allen, Frederick Lewis. *Only Yesterday: An Informal History of the 1920s.* New York: Harper and Row, 1931. http://xroads.virginia.edu/~hyper/allen/Cover.html.

American Elevator and Grain Trade, vol. 39, no. 8, 15 February, Chicago: Mitchell Brothers Publishing Co., 1921.

Austin, Dan. *Fisher Building*, HistoricDetroit.org. https://historicdetroit.org/ buildings/fisher-building.

Automotive Hall of Fame, https://www.automotivehalloffame.org/.

Baker, Bruce E., and Barbara Hahn. *The Cotton Kings: Capitalism and Corruption in Turn-of-the-Century New York and New Orleans*. New York: Oxford University Press, 2015.

Blumenthal, Karen. *Six Days in October: The Stock Market Crash of 1929*. New York: Atheneum, 2002.

Boettiger, John. "The Solution of the Lingle Murder." Series of articles in the *Chicago Tribune*, 5–29 April 1931.

Bowley, Pat. "Central, Torrance, Tytler and Victory Schools: Choosing a Name and Location." *Guelph Historical Society* 41 (2002): 25–35.

Brett, Frank. *Cutten Club 50th Anniversary Book*. Guelph, ON: Leaman Printing, 1981.

Brinkley, Alan. "When Washington Took On Wall Street." *Vanity Fair*, 17 May 2010. http://www.vanityfair.com/news/2010/06/pecora-201006.

Brooks, John. *Once in Golconda: A True Drama of Wall Street, 1920–1938*. New York: John Wiley and Sons, 1997.

– "The Millionaire and the Midget. *American Heritage* 20, no. 6 (1969). https://www.americanheritage.com/millionaire-midget.

Business Week. "Arthur Cutten, No In-and-Outer, Sees Real Merit in Grain Market." 18 November 1931.

Canada Directory for 1857–58. Montreal: John Lovell, 1957.

Canadian County Atlas Digital Project, http://digital.library.mcgill.ca/ countyatlas/default.htm.

Chase, William, ed. *The Delta Upsilon Quinquennial Catalogue*. Boston: The Delta Upsilon Fraternity, 1884.

Chernow, Ron. *The House of Morgan: An American Banking Dynasty and the Rise of Modern Finance*. New York: Grove/Atlantic, 2010.

Chrysler, Walter P., with Boyden Sparkes. *Life of an American Workman*. New York: Dodd, Mead and Company, 1950. https://gutenberg.ca/ebooks/ chrysler-workman/chrysler-workman-00-h-dir/chrysler-workman-00-h.html.

Clayton, H.J. *Clayton's Quaker Cook Book*. San Francisco: Women's Co-Operative Printing Office, 1883.

Cobban, Timothy W. *Cities of Oil: Municipalities and Petroleum Manufacturing in Southern Ontario, 1860–1960*. Toronto: University of Toronto Press, 2013.

Colby, Gerald. *Du Pont Dynasty: Behind the Nylon Curtain*. New York: Open Road Integrated Media, 1984. https://archive.org/stream/DupontDynasty/ Dupont%20Dynasty_djvu.txt.

Cooke, Frank H. "History of Woodlawn Cemetery." The Guelph Cemetery Commission, 1977.

Crowther, Samuel. "Everybody Ought To Be Rich: An Interview with John J. Raskob," *Ladies' Home Journal*, August 1929.

Cutten, Arthur W. with Boyden Sparkes. "The Story of a Speculator." *Saturday Evening Post,* 19 November, 26 November, 3 December, 10 December 1932.

Cutten, George Barton. *Genealogy of the Cutten Family of Nova Scotia.* Hamilton, New York: Colgate University, 1926.

Cutten, Lenore, and Peter Moore. *History of St George's Parish, Guelph.* Guelph, ON: Gummer Press, 1932.

DeLaurentis, Elysia. "Reminiscences of the 1870s in Guelph." *Guelph Historical Society* 42 (2003): 47.

Dies, Edward. *Street of Adventure.* Boston: Stratford Co., 1935.

DiGravio, Luke. "The Mystery of Arthur Cutten." *Guelph Historical Society* 41 (2002): 67–72.

Durant, Margery. *My Father.* New York: G.P. Putnam, 1929.

Elgin County Branch of the Ontario Genealogical Society. "County Places of Worship." Records Inventory, Bayham Township, 2006.

Elliott, Shirley B., ed. *The Legislative Assembly of Nova Scotia, 1758–1983: A Biographical Directory.* Province of Nova Scotia, 1984. https://archive.org/details/legislativeassem0000unse/page/n7/mode/1up?q=cutten.

Evans, Charles (Chick) Jr. *Chick Evans Golf Book.* Chicago: Published for Thos. E. Wilson & Co. by The Reilly & Lee Co., 1921.

Farber, David. *Everybody Ought to Be Rich: The Life and Times of John J. Raskob, Capitalist.* New York: Oxford University Press, 2013.

Ferris, William. *The Grain Traders: The Story of the Chicago Board of Trade.* East Lansing: Michigan State University Press, 1988.

Fetherling, George. *Gold Diggers of 1929: Canada and the Great Stock Market Crash.* Mississauga, ON: J. Wiley and Sons Canada, 2004.

Fisher, Gary L. "William C. 'Billy' Durant: The Man Who Invented the Future." Genesee County Historical Society, 2019. https://www.geneseehistory.org/william-c-durant.html.

Fisher, Kenneth. *100 Minds That Made the Market.* John Wiley and Sons, 2007.

Folsom, Burton W. "Billy Durant: From Carriages to Cars – How Family and Entrepreneurship Blended to Create the Largest Car Company in the World." Foundation for Economic Freedom, 1 March 1998. https://fee.org/articles/billy-durant-from-carriages-to-cars.

Forbes, B.C. *Men Who Are Making America.* New York: B.C. Forbes Publishing Co., 1917. https://ia800506.us.archive.org/21/items/menwhoaremakinga00for/menwhoaremakinga00for.pdf.

Galbraith, John Kenneth. *The Great Crash, 1929.* 50th anniversary ed. Boston: Houghton Mifflin Company, 1979.

Geisst, Charles. *Wall Street: A History from Its Beginnings to the Fall of Enron.* New York: Oxford University Press, 2004.

– *Wheels of Fortune: The History of Speculation from Scandal to Respectability.* New York: Wiley, 2002.

Goodspeed, W.A., and C.L. Goodspeed. *History of the County of Middlesex, Canada.* London, ON: Free Press Printing Company, 1889.

Gresham, Daniel T. "Reshaping the US Cattle Industry: Producers and Packers, 1914–1933." Diss. abstract, Kansas State University, 2019.

Greising, David, and Laurie Morse. *Brokers, Bagmen, and Moles: Fraud and Corruption in the Chicago Futures Markets.* New York: John Wiley and Sons Inc., 1991.

Gustin, Lawrence. *Billy Durant: Creator of General Motors.* Ann Arbor: University of Michigan Press, 2008.

Hahin, Bonnie. "The Hidden History of Hidden Lake." Hidden Lake Forest Preserve, Preserve Feature, Fall 2002, 3.

Hubert, J.J. *Archives of Cutten Fields.* Cutten Fields Golf Club, 2011.

Huertas, Thomas F., and Joan L. Silverman. "Charles E. Mitchell: Scapegoat of the Crash?" *Business History Review* 60, no. 1 (1986): 81–103.

Ingham, John. *Biographical Dictionary of American Business Leaders.* Vol. 1. Westport, CT: Greenwood Press, 1983.

Jacobus, John. *The Fisher Body Craftsman's Guild: An Illustrated History.* Jefferson (NC) and London: McFarland and Company, 2005.

Jenkins, Charles. "Lone Wolf of the Wheat Pit." *Maclean's,* 1 July 1922.

Johnson, Leo. *History of Guelph, 1827–1927.* Guelph Historical Society, 1977.

Keleher, John W. "Building Guelph's Railroads." *Guelph Historical Society* 34 (1994–95): 47–72.

King, Gilbert. "The Man Who Busted the Banksters." Smithsonianmag.com, November 2011. https://www.smithsonianmag.com/history/the-man-who-busted-the-banksters-932416/.

Klein, Maury. *Rainbow's End: The Crash of 1929.* New York: Oxford University Press, 2001.

Krajicek, David. "Corrupt Chicago Tribune Newsman Jake Lingle Gunned Down by Mafia Thug." *New York Daily News,* 8 June 2013.

Larson, Erik. *The Devil in the White City: Murder, Magic and Madness at the Fair That Changed America.* New York: Crown Publishers, 2003.

Lefevre, Edwin. *Reminiscences of a Stock Operator.* New York: George H. Doran Company, 1923.

Lough, David. *No More Champagne: Churchill and His Money.* New York: Picador, 2015.

Markham, Jerry. *A Financial History of the United States.* Vol. 2: *From J.P. Morgan to the Institutional Investor.* Armonk, NY: M.E. Sharpe, 2002.

– *Law Enforcement and the History of Financial Market Manipulation*. New York: Routledge, 2014.

– "Manipulation of Commodity Futures Prices – The Unprosecutable Crime." *Yale Journal on Regulation* 8 (1991): 281–389.

Maynard, W. Barksdale. "Archmere." In *Society of Architectural Historians*, ed. Gabrielle Esperdy and Karen Kingsley. Charlottesville: University of Virginia Press, 2012. http://sah-archipedia.org/buildings/DE-01-BR4.

McCarter, Robert. *Frank Lloyd Wright*. London: Phaidon Press, 1997.

McElvaine, Robert. *The Great Depression: America 1929–1941*. New York Times Books, 1984.

Meehan, Terence. *My American Story*. https://www.thecommongoodus.org/my-american-story-posts/my-american-story-terence-meehan.

Montague, Pat. "Guelph's Wheat King: Arthur Cutten." *Wellington Business Digest* 1, no. 5 (1985).

Mulvany, C. Pelham. *Toronto Past and Present: A Handbook of the City*. Toronto: W.E. Caiger, 1884.

Nations, Scott. *A History of the United States in Five Crashes: Stock Market Meltdowns That Defined a Nation*. New York: HarperCollins, 2017.

Naylor, R.T. *The History of Canadian Business, 1867–1914*. Toronto: J. Lorimer, 1975.

Neill, Humphrey B. *The Inside Story of the Stock Exchange, a Fascinating Saga of the World's Greatest Money Market Place*. New York: Forbes, 1950.

Niemeyer, Glen A., and James J. Flink. "The General of General Motors." *American Heritage* 24, no. 5 (1973). https://www.americanheritage.com/general-general-motors#1.

Parker, John Lloyd. *Unmasking Wall Street*. Boston: The Stratford Company, 1932.

Pasley, Fred. *Al Capone: The Biography of a Self-Made Man*. Garden City, NY: Garden City Publishing Company, 1930.

Patten, James. "In the Wheat Pit." *Saturday Evening Post*, 3 September, 17 September, 1 October, 15 October, 5 November, 19 November 1927.

Pecora, Ferdinand. *Wall Street under Oath: The Story of Our Modern Money Changers*. New York: Simon and Schuster, 1939.

Perino, Michael. *The Hellhound of Wall Street*. Penguin Publishing Group, Kindle ed.

Pollard, Ruth. "Guelph's Building Operations of 1877." *Guelph Historical Society* 29 (1990): 34–55.

Pound, Arthur. *The Turning Wheel: The Story of General Motors through Twenty-Five Years, 1908–1933*. Garden City, NY: Doubleday, 1934. https://ia902708.us.archive.org/13/items/turningwheelstoroopounrich/turningwheelstoroopounrich_bw.pdf.

Reynolds, Cate. "The History and Significance of John Jakob Raskob (1879-1950) and Pioneer Point." *What's Up Media*, 14 September 2017, https://whatsupmag.com/culture/history-significance-john-jakob-raskob-1879-1950-pioneer-point/.

Rollinson, Brenda. "The Spirit Walk at Woodlawn Cemetery: History Comes Alive!" *Guelph Historical Society* 41 (2002): 73–9.

Rubython, Tom. *Jesse Livermore – Boy Plunger: The Man Who Sold America Short in 1929*. Dorset, UK: Myrtle Press, 2015.

Sarnoff, Paul. *Jesse Livermore – Speculator-King*. Greenville, SC: Traders Press, 1985.

Savage, Edgar. "The Private Vengeance of Arthur Cutten." In *Real Detective Tales and Mystery Stories*, 26 April 1930.

Sharp, Robert. *The Lore and Legends of Wall Street*. Homewood, IL: Dow Jones-Irwin, 1989.

Smitten, Richard. *Jesse Livermore: World's Greatest Stock Trader*. New York: John Wiley and Sons, 2001.

Sobel, Robert. *The Big Board: A History of the New York Stock Market*. New York: The Free Press, 1965.

– *The Great Bull Market: Wall Street in the 1920s*. New York: W.W. Norton and Co. Inc., 1968.

– *Inside Wall Street*. New York: Norton, 1977.

Sparling, Earl. *Mystery Men of Wall Street*. New York: Greenberg, 1930.

Taylor, Charles Henry. *History of the Board of Trade of the City of Chicago*. 3 vols. Chicago: Robert O. Law Company, 1917.

Thomas, Gordon, and Max Morgan-Witts. *The Day the Bubble Burst: A Social History of the Wall Street Crash of 1929*. Garden City, NY: Doubleday, 1979.

Thompson, Richard A. "Around the Arboretum." DuPage County Historical Society, 1981.

Thorning, Stephen. "The Guelph Banking Company: Days of Wide Open Banking." *Wellington Advertiser* (Fergus, Ontario), 4 February 2000.

– "Hayseed Capitalists: Private Bankers in Ontario." PhD diss., McMaster University, 1994.

– "Irregular Banking Practices Sent Guelph's Walter Cutten to Court." *Wellington Advertiser* (Fergus, Ontario), 11 February 2000.

Veneziani, Vincent W. *The Greatest Trades of All Time: Top Traders Making Big Profits from the Crash of 1929 to Today*. Hoboken, NJ: Wiley, 2011.

INDEX